JAMES MAY
CAR FEVER

The car bore's essential companion

HODDER

To SFfD

The contents of this book first appeared in James May's
Daily Telegraph and *Top Gear Magazine* columns.

This edition is abridged from the original 2010 edition.

First published in Great Britain in 2009 by
Hodder & Stoughton
An Hachette UK company

First published in paperback in 2010

1

A CIP catalogue record for this title is available from the British Library.

ISBN 978 1 444 77934 9

Typeset in Excelsior by Palimpsest Book Production Limited,
Falkirk, Stirlingshire

Printed and bound by CPI Group (UK) Ltd, Croydon CR0 4YY

Hodder & Stoughton policy is to use papers that are natural, renewable
and recyclable products and made from wood grown in sustainable forests.
The logging and manufacturing processes are expected to conform to the
environmental regulations of the country of origin.

Hodder & Stoughton Ltd
338 Euston Road
London NW1 3BH

www.hodder.co.uk

Introduction

I feel that a book full of secondhand newspaper columns about motoring should begin with an apology, so here goes.

I'd like to apologise for that shirt I'm wearing on the cover. I know, from reading comments on the electric interweb, that many people feel quite strongly about that shirt, log its appearances on TV, discuss its sartorial merits, and implore me to get rid of it. But it isn't that simple.

You will see, if you read 'Old bag dies after 25 years as my friend' on page 165, that I had hitherto regarded my deceased Adidas rucksack as my constant fabric companion on this uncharted journey we call life. I now realise that it was the shirt.

That shirt is now me. It is the means by which my friends recognise me, and next to which my face performs only a secondary reserve role. It would be missed if it wasn't there.

Other shirts come and go quite quickly, because they shrink, tear, get left in hotels, sustain a curry injury, and so on. But this shirt refuses to give up its shirty duties. It has at least two holes in it, it's pretty threadbare, and the cuffs are badly frayed, but it just carries on. One day I will cough and it will turn into a puff of vapour to be carried away on the breeze, but until then I might as well wear it.

I could never discard a perfectly good shirt, or even a perfectly awful one if it still fits and covers up my unsightly nipples. My cleaner has taken the executive decision to turn other old shirts of mine into dusters and car polishing rags, but I have expressly forbidden her ever to do such a thing to this one.

It is the first shirt I ever bought specifically for TV appearances, and has now lasted so long, and been to so many places around the world, that it has become talismanic, like a raven at a historic building. I now take this shirt on every trip, even if I don't actually intend to wear it. For *Top Gear's* North Pole trip I obviously had to pack a lot of noisy and unflattering cold weather protective clothing, but The Shirt was in my rucksack all the same, to protect me.

A shirt, I suspect, is a little like a cat that is allowed to go outside. There's always the risk that it will be run over, but if it survives the first six months, then it's wise enough to survive into old age. Some shirts live only for a few glorious weeks before they are cruelly snatched away by the unforgiving and indiscriminate hand of shirt fate. This shirt has already lasted for six years of almost uninterrupted use, so I reckon it will be with me until the end.

At a rough guess, because even I'm not boring enough to keep a record of this sort of thing, this shirt has been washed and ironed over 500 times and has travelled at least 125,000 miles, or about half way to the moon. Yet by my calculations it is only one third of the way through its projected life, which means it should last for another 12 years. But I can easily eke that out to 15.

What really amazes me though, is that until I saw the cover design for this book, I hadn't really considered the significance of the blue flowery shirt in the formation of my character. I now realise that I don't really have any sort of job at all. Only my shirt does. I am not my body. I am not even my mind. I am merely the vessel that my shirt is wrapped around, and, as Oscar Wilde might have said, if this shirt goes, then so do I.

I hope you enjoy the motoring adventures of the blue flowery shirt as much as my shirt enjoyed writing it.

May's Britain, a broad sunlit upland

When I'm in power, there are going to be some changes around here, I can tell you. May's Britain is going to be a better place to live.

It's all a matter of passing some very simple and patently quite overdue laws. For a start, there will be strict penalties for any eating establishment that serves normal food in a bowl, and indeed for anyone who writes 'eating establishment' instead of 'restaurant'.

Now: food in a bowl is quite acceptable if it's one of those one-utensil, one-implement meals. Some pastas, for example; chilli con carne, cornflakes, stew, Spam and beans. But anyone caught presenting a pork chop and vegetables in something clearly intended for soup will go to prison for one year.

Similarly, the proprietor of any local who arranges sausage and mash in an artful way, instead of forming the mash into a neat Mount Fuji and inserting the sausages into it in the style of the *Dandy*, will be made to eat pizza and work in a municipal scullery until he or she renounces gastropubbery. No one can deny that this will make the country a better place.

And it's not just about food; there's more, from the field of retail. This week, with a mate, I have tried camping for the first time in many years, and, having disposed of my childhood tent long ago in a part-exchange deal against some bicycle spares, decided to buy a new one.

The man in the camping shop described the one I eventually

chose (from a picture in a book) as a two-stroke-three-man tent.
I believed him. He may have believed it himself. But once it was
erected it became quite clear that it was barely big enough for
one normal bloke, or at a pinch two who like each other a lot.
It tapered towards one end, causing unwanted intimacy, and was
very low. Furthermore, the sleeping bag he sold me was also
tapered, and quite patently based on a sleep-deprivation torture
designed by Chairman Mao to make political prisoners confess.

Apparently, these features enhance the chances of survival
in sub-zero temperatures and howling winds on the north face
of a mountain. Yet the purveyor of tents must have known, when
he saw me, that I was the sort of man who never imagined that
a tent could be anything other than triangular in section, and
who would assume a sleeping bag to be rectangular.

Fine. In May's Britain he will be allowed to continue selling
such tents. But only after he has lived in one for six months.

See? Some simple rules based on jeopardy will cure our
society of many of its creeping blights while ridding it of the
hideous spectre of liability-based legislation. I'm not going to
concern myself with the funding of the health service, immi-
gration or the housing crisis. I'll use the appropriate experts
for these. I will just concentrate on those small, nagging irri-
tations that ruin our lives out of all proportion.

Here's another one. A man outside my window has just started
using one of those petrol-engine leaf-blowers. This is a truly
fatuous piece of kit. The leaves are all over his garden because
nature blew them there in the first place, and blowing them
around some more will achieve nothing other than the complete
ruination of my day. He's just making a horrible noise and
annoying everyone within a two-mile radius, which means he's
caused more distress in the community than a burglar who
merely robs one house. Prison. One year.

Obviously, I have some plans to make life better and fairer
for the motorist, too. I'm not going to clamp down on speed
cameras or road tolls, I'm not going to ban caravans, there will

be no punishment for driving in the middle lane of an empty motorway, and I'm not going to do anything at all about untaxed vehicles. These things are not bothering me much.

But traffic wardens seem to be more aggressive, more pedantic, and more superior than ever. The 'parking enforcement officer' has become almost untouchable in Britain, and has been elevated to some spurious moral high ground that brooks no contest and admits no latitude. So I have a plan.

If you apply for a job as a traffic warden, you will immediately be sent to one of my new prisons. There you will sew mail bags, slop out for your colleagues, and take part in a weekly day-release programme of community service activities to help the old, the infirm, and the disadvantaged.

And when you have proved yourself to be honest, socially upstanding and of spotless character, you will be released, given a hat, and permitted to stand in judgement on others' fallibility.

But not before.

Italian engine, charismatic, would like to meet small Japanese sports car for shed frolics

A car I still admire, even after the twelve years that have passed since I had one as a company car in a proper job that I went to every day, is the Alfa Romeo 164 3.0 V6.

Even if you noticed them at the time, you may have forgotten that the 164 ever existed. There certainly aren't many of them around any more, and whenever I've tried to find a good one during an attack of car fever, I've only ever been able to locate a complete snotter. So I forgot about the 164 as well.

But then, a few weeks ago, we devised another of our *Top Gear* challenges; one of those that requires us each to buy a car for £1000. I suggested – silly, really – that I'd quite like an Alfa Romeo 164 3.0. So the researchers, who are pretty good at this sort of thing, went to work on the World Wide Web of Lies and came up with a tidy-looking top-spec Cloverleaf model even before I'd got back from the newsagents with *Autotrader*.

So we bought it, I took it for a drive, and it's still pretty good. The undercarriage of this 170,000-miler was perhaps a bit sloppy, and I'm sure the gearchange was crisper on the one I had, but it was still quite magical. What's more, and contrary to the reputation old Alfas have, everything on it still worked: the air-con, the curious keyboard controls for the fan and heater, the interior lights, the seat motors – the lot. The interior was excellent.

Next, we put it up on ramps and had a good look around

underneath. Very solid. No leaks. No signs of crash damage. I found a small patch of rot, about the size of my thumb, where a door seal had perished and created a water trap, but it represented no more than two hundred pounds worth of repair work. Here, at last, was a good Alfa 164.

And so, in accordance with the rules of the challenge, I sawed it in two. From a technical point of view this was quite difficult, and I was obliged to wear some safety glasses in case I was hit in the eye by half a car. It was even more difficult emotionally, as I wanted to keep it the way its maker had intended and even in my garage.

Exactly why I had to saw it in half I can't tell you, because it's secret and I don't want to spoil the forthcoming moment of 'TV comedy gold' when it rolls on to your screens*. You can be reasonably certain, though, that the whole episode will not end elegantly and that the two halves of the 164 will never be satisfactorily reunited. I'm fairly heartbroken.

On the other hand, I do know the rules of this competition and I'm fairly confident that the best bit of the 164, the engine, will survive. And this had me thinking. A week later I drove an original Mazda MX-5 around a small racing circuit, and was reminded of what a great car it is. Then I wondered how much better it would be with the Alfa engine installed.

Would it fit? The wit of man when it comes to forcing things into places where they weren't designed to go – anchovies inside olives, for example – knows no bounds. From a practical and geometric point of view, my piano should never have made it up my dog-legged staircase and into my sitting room. But it did and so, under the terms of the deal I struck with the piano shop, I had to buy it.

I really like the idea. The balance and rear-drive response of the little Japanese roadster, the vivacity and muscle of Italy's most charismatic V6. I'm sure there would be a few

---

*It became one half of my Alfa-Saab push-me-pull-you limo.

dimensional and weight issues, but it's no more ridiculous than shoe-horning a big V8 into the AC Ace to make the Cobra, or yet another big V8 into the Sunbeam Alpine to make the Tiger. It must be possible.

Of course, Mazda or Alfa Romeo would never consider such a thing. They're rivals, they have no tie-ups, and the process would be fraught with the sort of legal and logistical obstacles that only massive corporations can put in their own paths.

But Britain is festooned with the sort of business that thrives on this sort of thing. I'm not talking about Lotus or Prodrive, or even Williams engineering. I mean men in sheds.

Men in sheds were the cornerstone of this nation's industrial greatness, and men in sheds are its most enduring legacy. They're still there, mending, making, inventing and confronting accepted practice. Some of them are even making cars, and one of them could build me a Mazda Romeo.

Morgan, I mean you.

Old things – not as good as they once were

A common feature in a Sunday newspaper supplement is the one in which some person of significance describes his or her typical day. You know the sort of thing: get up at such and such a time, unlock the kids' bedroom, eat this, do that, meet these people, and so on.

These articles drive me up the wall. For one thing, no one important ever seems to do anything, which makes me wonder how they came to be so influential that a newspaper wants to talk to them. Secondly, they're always thinly disguised boasts about how Fairtrade the coffee is, or how sophisticated the home appliances. There's always far too much mention of the juicer for my liking.

So, by way of contrast, I bring you a life in the Sunday of a slightly sad middle-aged bloke with a debilitating enthusiasm for mechanical items powered by internal combustion engines. It's not good and is intended as a warning.

The plan was simple. Make my way to the local flying club, using one of the nine modes of personal transport available to me, and go for a flip in the tenth, my little light aircraft. So we begin in the garage with my modest collection of classic motorcycles.

Most recent addition to this lot is my 1968 Honda CB250 twin. I like old Hondas a lot, and had been looking for one of these for a bit. Eventually I found one that a bloke had restored beautifully but couldn't make run properly, and so, exploiting his despair, I knocked him down substantially on the asking price on the basis that I'd be able to sort it back home.

And I did, after about three months, eventually tracing the fault to a tiny missing rubber bung inside one of the carburettors. The 250 burst into life, after a spot of fooling about with jump leads and a booster pack. It was even running on both cylinders! So off I went.

But within a mile I was rewarded with a damp leg, the result of petrol spouting from the carb assembly like some ornamental fuel fountain. But not to worry, because I have two more old Hondas. My early-60s C200, for example; a simple machine of 90cc and an uplifting, prosaic experience. The least a motorcycle can be while still technically being one. This turned out to be as dead as Jacob Marley in *A Christmas Carol*, that is, as a doornail.

So I turned to the 1972 CB500 Four, one of the finest products ever to come from Soichiro Honda's bid for two-wheeled world domination. After reassembling it and extracting it from the back of the garage, I pressed the starter button and something exploded in the bowels of its complex four-pot motor. But at least moving that out of the way had given me access to the Moto Guzzi V11, which I've owned from new for many years and maintained fastidiously.

Obviously that didn't work, because it was built near Lake Como in northern Italy, a place famous for ice-cream and ancient chapels dedicated to St Anthony, the patron saint of things that are lost. So finally, after several hours of trying, I was forced onto the seat of my Triumph Speed Triple which, being new, started immediately.

But then Woman turned up and demanded to be taken to the airfield as well, and as she hates motorcycles this meant turning my attention to the cars. The old Bentley is a nice way to travel on a sunny day of fun, but technically it's for sale as I've bought an old Rolls-Royce instead. And the fuel gauge is broken. Meanwhile, the Royce isn't here yet because it's away with a man who's re-lacquering the cracked dashboard, after which it's in for some engine work.

The Porsche, then. It's my poshest car and a convertible to boot, and just the sort of thing in which a chap and his gal might arrive at an airfield. No, not the Porsche, because one of the windows has stuck in the open position so it can't be parked anywhere. And so, some three hours after I stepped out of my front door, we set off in the Fiat Panda.

And it didn't end there. At the airfield, I uncovered my Luscombe 8 monoplane, an American-built machine of 1946 vintage. In its time, it was a radical aeroplane, the first all-metal light aircraft, something that could live outdoors without fear of the wings rotting away or anything like that. It is in excellent condition and has been rigorously serviced for its entire life, as you would demand of an aircraft.

I spent the usual half a lifetime on my pre-flight checks, fuelled up, strapped in and ran through the start-up procedure. The 100hp air-cooled flat-four roared into lustful life. I taxied to the end of the runway, did some more checks for full power, oil pressure and all the rest of it and then opened the throttle.

Halfway down the runway I was rewarded with what I regard as a porthole to the sublime; a view of a perfect English heaven, seen through the screen of a classic aeroplane in the moment it lifts from the grass at the historic White Waltham airfield. And then, at 800 feet, the engine cut out. Not permanently – it just faltered for a few seconds and then picked up again – but even so I nearly soiled myself. Five minutes later I was back on the deck covering it up again.

The message here is quite simple. All this old stuff is rubbish. None of it works properly. After almost a whole day of fart-arsing around with machinery I was forced to conclude that the only dependable things in my life are an Italian car and a British motorcycle. No one would have bet on that.

And here's the advice. Buy one new car, any car, and use that for everything. Then you can devote the rest of your life to something useful.

How not to drive like an Italian

As I've always understood things, there is only one way to drive a small Fiat; and that is without mercy.

Here's how to do it. Select first, lift the clutch abruptly, mash the throttle pedal to the floor and when, and only when, the valve gear bursts through the bonnet, select second. Repeat the process until all the gears are used up.

A small Fiat will thank you for this, because that's what it was designed for. The original Cinquecento, the 124, the 126, the 127, the first Panda, the Uno, the Tipo, the second Cinquecento and the Seicento – they all gave of their best when they were giving of their all. You may not actually have gone very fast, but that is the Italian way – noise, drama, quite a lot of arm waving but very little actually being achieved. It was endlessly entertaining and endearing, like a waiter's arithmetic in the Lira Era.

I have a small Fiat, a Panda. I love it. The 1.2-litre engine may as well be set up to idle at 4000rpm, because using any less than that is an affront to the memory of Dante Giacosa, the man who showed us the way forward with the original Fiat 500. Drive a good one of these and you will never believe that a car is underpowered. Power per se is not the point; it is the nature of the performance that counts, and the 500 had the heart of Caruso.

This brings me to the new Fiat 500, which I've just been driving. Like the Mini and the Mustang, it leaves me a little uneasy, because I don't think pastiches of old cars work very well. The design language of the 1950s does not sit comfortably with the demands we make of a modern car; for airbags, electric windows, crash-worthiness, rollover protection, proper seats, and so on. In an original 500 it doesn't matter that the windows are so small – because you sit so close to them, and because the side of the car is only the thickness of a stout coat away from your shoulder, the bodywork impairs the vision no more than the frames of a pair of specs would. But the new one is too big for its shape and actually feels more claustrophobic as a result. Visibility is quite poor, and the chunky interior trim seems to crowd the cabin and leave it bereft of air and light.

However, I accept that this is largely a matter of fashion, and I acknowledge wholeheartedly that I am not in a position to comment on such things, as what I know about fashion could be written on the label in my brown sports jacket. In any case, the 500 is merely a Panda like mine under its shamelessly nostalgic skin, so at least it would be a hoot to drive.

Imagine my dismay, horror, abject misery, self-doubt, spiritual paralysis and even downright disappointment when I turned the key and discovered that I'd been sent the *diesel* version. I've never known an engine so ill-matched to the imagined temperament of the car to which it is fitted, and the human psyche does not admit of a demon more chilling than that conjured up by the unexpected clatter of compression ignition.

I can just about accept the dieselists' argument for Rudolf's evil invention in a large luxury car, where low-range torque can ultimately add to the sense of sophistication and calm. The petrol V8 in my old Rolls-Royce is a diesel to all intents and purposes – it redlines at 4500rpm and I've never used more than about 3500. It doesn't bother me.

But in a small car? Never. A small diesel does the job for you, but a small petrol engine demands that you enter a pact in which you must work together for the furtherance of meagre performance. The diesel grumbles and has bad breath; the petrol squeals with delight and is as fragrant as one of John Donne's mistresses. Who, in fact, could possibly even consider specifying the new Fiat 500, a car built in honour of the most under-endowed but effusive Fiat of all time, with a diesel engine? Why is this noisome instrument of the eternally tiresome even offered? Here is a spiritual sprite amongst cars, and only a serial miserablist would want it propelled by the heel-dragging drudge that is a diesel.

I know a lot of you are interested in this car. I know, too, that the diesel propaganda machine is a persuasive one. Just say no. Of course the diesel model will work out cheaper than the petrol one in the long run, but so it should. It's not as good.

And yes, there's some chance that you will melt the petrol engine, but it's all in a good cause. You'll be saving the soul of Italy.

Not to mention a large chunk of your own.

The rot stops here

Not for the first time in history, the motor industry is in a position to show the rest of commerce the way forward.

It's happened before. Henry Ford may not have actually invented mass production – we can look to the clock and gunsmithing businesses for that – but he did show that something formerly considered totally inaccessible to the normal people could actually be affordable.

In the 50s and 60s cars showed that high style and fashion could be had in an everyday consumer durable. They also encouraged the acceptance of new materials such as plastic, vinyl and even – in the door trims of the Rover P6 – Formica. More recently, and despite what the miserablists would tell you, car manufacturers have led the way in improving the dependability of the product as well as the efficiency of the means by which it is produced.

But there's still more to be done, so now I'd like to have a look at shops. When I was a small boy, shops were pretty much the way they had been since the turn of the century, which was usually closed. If they weren't closed, there was a good chance they wouldn't have what you wanted, even if it did all cost a penny.

Sadly, I'm old enough to remember the advent of the supermarket, at least up in t'north where I was living. I mean real supermarkets; huge Sainsbury's with great Babel-like towers of fruit and bog roll stretching away to eternity. I loved the supermarket when I went there with my mum to stock up for our family of six: its inconceivable inventory of stuff from all over the world, all under one roof and seemingly always open.

I still like a good supermarket, but these days it's just me and Fusker the cat, and there's the problem. It's a bit facile driving two miles to the great grocer's colossus to stand in line with my meagre basket of Whiskas and pies. A smaller, closer shop would do.

Sainsbury's realised as much, and now provides a miniature supermarket only half the distance away of the big one and probably only about a twentieth the size. Tesco have gone even further. They have really big Tescos in the wilderness, quite big Tescos on the edge of towns and town-centre Tescos called Tesco Metro. And now, at the end of my road and on the site of a former petrol station, is Tesco Local. I can almost shop there in loose robes.

But it's still not enough, because I go to Tesco, buy things, then bring them home and store them in my own cupboards. No matter how localised the supermarkets seem, there is still, in effect, an even more local one in a corner of my kitchen. Here, food goes off.

The car-making business would never allow this, because for years it has been working to the principle of 'just in time', which means that a factory carries no significant stock of parts and that all components are delivered terrifyingly close to the point in time when they will be needed.

Take Ford's Michigan Truck Plant, where its big 4x4s are assembled. An articulated lorry from a seat supplier will roll up at one door of the factory building. Its tarpaulin sides are lowered, and there, in the trailer, are enough seats for maybe three cars. They are in sets of different colours, and stacked in the correct order. They are simply loaded onto a branch of the moving assembly line and, by some miracle, end up in the right position in the right cars. This happens constantly throughout the day.

Wheels arrive at Mazda's Hofu plant in the same way. On this line, everything from a small sports car to a large panel van is made, and wheels for all of them arrive in small batches in some uncharted corner of the complex. But with minimal intervention, they all end up on the right vehicles. If it went wrong once, every car thereafter would be wrong. But it's always right, and I've never seen an MX-5 running around on the wheels from a Bongo Friendy van.

How this industrial brinkmanship is effected is one of the great mysteries of the modern world, but effected it is, and the space and overheads associated with sitting on piles of parts are saved. Once, in one of Toyota's factories, I was truly appalled at the tiny number of mounting screws available at any one time to a man whose job it was to fit headlights to Corollas. But every time I looked again, the little tub containing them had been replenished. Later in the day I discovered that I'd inadvertently put one of these screws in my pocket, and spent the night worrying that I'd brought the whole Japanese industrial engine to a shuddering and screwless halt.

Back to the local shop, where sausages are still sold in packs of six when I only want two. I buy six, and leave four in the fridge to rot. Why? Someone should hand me two sausages in the last yawning moment before I fire up the frying pan. And that gives me an idea.

I have in mind a new kitchen cupboard, one that opens into the house but also out onto the street, guarded by a simple security device. If I decide I want a fryup, I simply turn to my computer and enter exactly what I need. Ten minutes later, when I step into the kitchen and open my just-in-time cupboard, the ingredients are there: two sausages, two rashers of bacon, one egg, one piece of bread for the toast, half a tomato, two heaped teaspoonsfuls of baked beans, and a small sachet of brown sauce. How they get there I need not worry, and I need never worry that they won't be there either, just as headlight man doesn't need to fret about screw supplies.

This wouldn't be too difficult to arrange. Supermarkets already deliver, but they deliver huge piles of food that then go into a fridge, which is something Nissan would never tolerate, and rightly so. They've just come from a fridge. Why put them in another one? My scheme represents salvation for the bachelor and would free large families from the tyranny of trying to decide on Saturday what they might want to eat on the following Friday. And without the need for a fridge or all those tiresome cupboards, the kitchen can be smaller and a more agreeable room, such as the garage, a little bigger.

Apparently Honda is quite flush these days. Perhaps it could buy up Spar and set to work.

Join the police and look really stupid

Two bits of interesting reading this week. The first was an article in the *Daily Telegraph* about the future of British police transport, and the other was Mad Frankie Fraser's *Underworld History of Britain*.

On the whole, I preferred Mad Frank. I know the glorification of common criminals is supposed to be a bad thing, and I know he and his mates Cruncher and Scarface (or whatever they're called) are essentially bad men, but the trouble is that the crims come out looking a lot cooler than the rozzers. They're better paid as well, although they can only spend it in Spain.

I sense a looming crisis in police recruitment, and I'm afraid it's largely down to the image of the profession. If you're a ned, you at least get a crowbar or a knuckle duster as an entry-level badge of office, and if you turn out to be any good the firm might stretch to a dodgy drinking club in London's West End, where you'll occupy your own office with a couple of nice brasses on your desk. Join the police and you get . . . well, let's take a look.

The first sign of rot was the widespread adoption of fluorescent safety-style policewear. This makes the police look a bit soft in my view, because the impression is that the personal safety of police officers is more important than pursuing the miscreant in a westerly direction and apprehending Mad Frankie in the act of doing over a pawnbrokers.

Another worrying development has been modern police

sirens. When I was a boy the Allegro patrol car had a simple blue light and emitted an authoritative bee-baa-bee-baa noise that any child could imitate. Now police cars feature the light show from a Village People concert and the whoopsie siren can only be impersonated by someone who almost got the lead role in *Some Mothers Do 'Ave 'Em*.

I'm worried that the police are being made to look a bit soft. Around here, whoever is in charge of plod has obviously been suckered into the 'branding' movement during a meeting with Bogarty Bowtie Bowtie Braces and Spectacles, and police vehicles display a legend that reads something like 'Working together in the community to raise awareness of understanding' (it's not that, but you know what I mean). I'd have 'The police – protecting you from the oiks'.

And now look – the T3 electric three-wheel vehicle. With the best will in the world, the policeman depicted riding on this thing just looks bloody silly, and you'd have no qualms about knocking his helmet off with a catapult. The boss of the company making it says the T3 has the 'wow factor', but when I look at it the sound that springs involuntarily from my lips is 'why?'

There are a few obvious drawbacks with this thing. Firstly, it has three wheels, and very few things with three wheels work properly. Secondly, you stand up to drive it. Even Karl Benz worked out that it was better to sit down.

The T3 has a top speed of 25mph, which sounds pretty good for an electric vehicle, but that's the problem. We've become so used to the dismal performance of anything battery-powered that we're impressed by even the most feeble performance figures. The fact remains that a MkII 3.8 Jag or a hooky 1600E Cortina is still a lot faster, especially in the hands of Nosher or Fingers. Yes, the T3 will mount kerbs, but so will a policeman's legs; and it won't go off road, so you don't need to be a criminal mastermind to work out which way to leg it when surprised by the bill. An electric three-wheeled vehicle is a device for allowing fat Americans to cross a shopping mall, not a front-line weapon in the fight against crime.

The sad fact is that whenever I talk to a normal bobby or traffic cop, they quickly admit that they hate all this sort of stuff. So I've come up with a much better urban police rapid response transportation system solution.

A few weeks back I bought a new Triumph Speed Triple. I was intending to have a black one, but once in the showroom I discovered that it looked very good in white, so had that instead. I think my Speed Triple has the makings of a really impressive police bike, having the power, the agility, and the correct Raffles the Gentleman Thug image to strike fear into the hearts of telly-pinching pikeys everywhere.

All they need to do is scrub out 'Triumph' on the petrol tank and substitute 'Police'. Then they need to send all the policeman to the Rocket Ron Haslam racing school, where they can learn to get it right over. Respect restored.

A postcard from France, part I

Dear readers,

I write to you from La Belle France, where I have now been for four whole days. The weather has been glorious for three of them, but very bad on the evening of the one on which we decided to camp for the night. *C'est la vie*, though normally only in the Lake District.

In case you weren't reading three weeks ago, when I was still on the Main Land, I am here for a month to make a six-part series for BBC2 on the subject of French wine. I know nothing about French wine, or indeed any other type of wine, but that's the whole point. I am accompanied by Oz 'woody finish' Clarke, the idea being that his immense and largely inaccessible knowledge of the subject will be filtered through my own ignorance and general peevishness until it is in a form palatable to normal folk who simply want a half-decent bottle of grog to knock back with the rosbif.

To that end I bought a 17-year-old Jaguar XJ-S V12 convertible, partly in the hope that it would do the decent old-Jag thing and leave me stranded in Kent, where I could just have a nice pint instead. Sadly, no. It has so far brought us all the way to Bordeaux. This is in part the fault of Knowles-Wilkins Engineering, purveyors of subtly refettled XJ-S and Series 3 Jaguars, who worked continuously on the car from the day I bought it to the evening of the day before I left.

So on this trip I have two friendships to cultivate. One with my new car, the other with Oz 'nectarine high notes' himself. And there is no better way to bond with either a car or another chap than on a proper, epic road trip.

It's a while since I drove an XJ-S. Much of it is as glorious as it ever was: the silken swelling that comes only with a full-bodied and robust petrol V12, the challenging complexity of the under-bonnet arrangement, the satisfying vintage of its green LED trip computer, and the woody finish on the dashboard.

In other ways it serves to remind us how far cars have come since this one was conceived, and convertibles in particular. The vogue for the so-called coupe-cabrio, a type of car with a solid folding roof now espoused by Vauxhall, VW, Daihatsu, Renault, Peugeot, Mercedes, Mitsubishi et al, may cause us to forget that there was a time, not so long ago, when the folded fabric roof of a large GT drophead would sit on top of the boot like the remains of the R101 airship disaster; or that the owner was expected to step outside and shroud the wreckage with an ill-fitting cloth cover that attaches by means of 1001 poppers and hooks, so that the collapsed mechanism can be disguised as a 70s sofa instead. I infer from the near-pristine condition of this 'hood bag', which takes up much valuable space in the boot, that the previous owner couldn't really be bothered. And neither, it transpires, can I.

But the old Jag is still a great car. Hopeless on the autoroute it may be – the wind wails in the gaps around the hood, the fuel consumption is atrocious, and it has the torsional rigidity of a piano accordion – but top-down on a winding D-road it has greatly endeared itself to me.

I wish I could say the same about Oz. For the last three days he has attempted to educate me in 'the vocabulary of wine' by shoving a variety of organic items – nettles, cinnamon sticks, garlic, cow poo, cashew nuts, apples, oranges, vinegar – under my nose and demanding that I 'learn' their smells. This in itself wouldn't be so bad, but all these things are now in the passenger footwell of my newly re-carpeted XJ-S, which he treats like the skip round the back of the *Ready Steady Cook* studio. *Vive la différence* is all very well, but this bloke is filling my new car with rotting fruit and spoiling the mature and musty nose of the interior. I wouldn't mind if I got a drink occasionally, but since I'm always driving I can only really commend to you the 2006 Badoit mineral water. Sparkling.

So – he gets to drink a 1988 Chateau Baron Bomburst at £75 a bottle, and I get to drive around in a 17-year-old Jaguar. Still, it could be worse. It could be the other way round.

More in a week or so.

Bon nuit,

James

The strange case of the missing Panda

A while back, I lost a pair of my trousers. Nothing too trau-
matic about that – I have another pair – but what perplexes
me is how this could have happened. It's perfectly easy to leave
a jacket, a scarf or a hat somewhere, but trousers? That they
are nowhere in the house must mean I went out with trousers
on and then came home in my pants.

It gets worse. Yesterday, I went outside and discovered that
my Fiat Panda was missing. That must mean I drove it to the
shops, forgot I owned it and then came home on the bus.
Unlikely, even by my standards.

And anyway, it wouldn't be the first time I'd lost the car. On
more than one occasion I've timed a journey to the airport
allowing just five minutes for stylish brinkmanship, only to
open the front door and remember that, for complex reasons
usually involving drink, the Panda is in the BBC car park.

But it wasn't in the BBC car park. Neither was it round the
corner, and nor had it been removed by some of my 'humorous'
TV colleagues. I plotted its last movements and eventually had
to accept that it had been stolen. So I rang the police and took
some pleasure in saying that I needed to report a missing Panda.
But the woman on the other end of the phone didn't think that
was funny, or even that it constituted a genuine 999 emergency,
and advised me to ring the local cop shop instead. I now entered
a world of hitherto unimagined woe.

First I had to ring another company to obtain something

called a 'trace' code for the vehicle for yourself sir. Then I had to give this to the police, who took details of the car and its owner and gave me a crime reference number. Then I had to give this to my insurers, who emailed a complex claim form for me to fail to print out.

And then, finally, the police rang me back to say the Panda had been located – in the local car pound. Because I hadn't paid the road tax. One of several great things about the Panda is that, as a small and economical car, its annual road fund licence is discounted to just £117.50. Unless you're me, in which case it turns out to be £420.

Now you're probably thinking rules is rules and there isn't one for me and another for everyone else. But what bothers me about this is that, as a busy man with his nose pressed to the relentless grindstone of the Protestant work ethic, who had simply committed a small oversight and of course viewed the payment of tax as a civilising duty, I was being treated no differently from a common chancer who had no intention of paying at all. That the disc was two months out of date was a mere technicality and not a basis on which to besmirch my good character.

It would be more neighbourly, I pointed out to the man in the office of whichever contractor now deals with these things, to ring or write and gently remind the blameless and law-abiding middle-class citizen of his error. That the reminder was sitting in a vast pile of post I couldn't be bothered to open is neither here nor there.

And why, I have to ask, is an untaxed but otherwise road-legal car towed away without further ado, when something like a pre-emptive fine would have spurred me into action and saved a great deal of inconvenience and expense for everyone involved? Just because the towaway truck drives around with a siren blaring to give potential offenders an even chance is not really material, and the simple fact that the car was clamped for three days during which I could have paid the road fund licence with no further questions asked is merely an attempt to fudge the issue in question, which is that I'm being unfairly criminalised for a brief lapse into human fallibility.

And here's the bit that really enrages me. Having taken my car away, they didn't even bother to tell me. It might have been weeks before I noticed. Just because they wrote to me immediately is no sort of defence. They should have realised from the way I ignored the reminder that I don't open any of this stuff.

Once again the honest, upright and accountable people of Britain are being punished as an example to a criminal fraternity that couldn't care less. The agencies of law and order, lacking the balls or authority to deal with the real blights on society, imagine we will be fooled by the odd campaign to harass the very people who could be depended upon to support them. Or something like that. Soon, we will decide we've had enough of it, and we will rise up.

In the meantime, though, it might be worth checking that your tax disc is still current.

If the car fits, wear it

When I saw it on its hanger, I thought the yellow shirt with the green lozenge pattern and contrasting embroidery looked pretty good. I like a Lego palette in casual clothing, so I tried it on.

But when I looked in the shop mirror, I had to acknowledge that I looked a bit of a berk. I was a middle-aged man in a shirt obviously designed to complement the attitude of a feckless, shuffling youth with trousers hanging around his arse and an iPod playlist to match. So I put the shirt back on the rack and bought a brown jumper instead.

This brings me to the new Maserati GT. I really like the look of that car. I'm a bit of a fan of modern Masers in general, and especially of the later V8 engine with its muscle-car crank angles and subdued yet guttural exhaust note. Where Lambos and Ferraris are for footballers and pop stars, Maseratis are somehow far more discreet and generally driven by gentlemen and ripping gals. Sophia Loren had a Maserati, and so did the Shah of Persia. I like to think of myself as a Maserati kind of bloke.

But I could be wrong, and here we arrive at a potential pitfall for the modern motorist. I bet no car showroom in the country has a mirror in it, so how can I be sure I don't look a complete knob in the GT? Furthermore, while sales assistants in clothes shops will often be honest and tell you how much better you look in the plain blue one, I suspect a Subaru dealer would sell an Impreza to a man who walked in with a white stick.

Be honest: have you ever heard a car salesman say anything like 'I'm not sure you're really quite enough of a pikey to drive this particular model, madam,' or 'If you don't mind me saying so, sir, I think your face is a bit too circular for the BMW Z coupe. You have an enduringly comedic countenance, and this is an aggressive-looking car. May I suggest a Nissan Micra?' It doesn't happen, which is why I saw that very man driving such an ill-fitting BMW only yesterday.

I know, from observing as much in a large shop window, that I look as big a pillock in a Chrysler PT Cruiser as I would in a Sari. But that's not to say that you would. All we can know for certain is that the dealer won't help in this respect, so it's up to us.

I now realise how easy it is to get this wrong. I realise because my own Porsche is obviously a bit of a case in point judging by some of the comments I've overheard from bystanders. When I bought it, I didn't think to check—the Porsche dealer doesn't have a mirror either—but now I've had a good look in the window of John Lewis while stuck in a jam I can see that, while it's not quite as ridiculous as plus fours, it might be a bit borderline for the tatty T-shirt kind of chap that I really am.

It's so very tempting to imagine that the attributes of the car will automatically be assumed by you, the potential new owner. But it simply isn't true. Porsche has an enviable sporting pedigree, a history of uncompromising excellence, and a reputation for delivering peerless quality. But that won't actually make you any less fat, blotchy, and working in the financial services sector, so you will still look like a man who shouldn't have bought a 911. There are a lot of them around, I've noticed.

So to the man in the old E-type: you're too tall and your face is too thin. You should be in a Citroën DS. To the short man in the Seat Leon: this car's waistline is high, but yours isn't. You are a reasonably good-looking bloke and your car is quite rakish. But it looks as though it's being driven by a disembodied head on a stick. And to the woman in the Mercedes E-class diesel: your hair is too mad, and someone should have had the decency to tell you how much better a Land Rover Defender would have suited you.

Style, as I believe Samuel Wesley said, is the dress of thought, so it's worth checking your appearance before you go out. The other day I saw a serious-looking besuited bloke with neat hair driving a bright green Smart car. And I couldn't help but react in the way my mother does whenever she sees a man walking bare-chested around town.

Go and put a proper car on.

Thank you for buying an unfinished car

Something that's always bothered me about the car business is this: why can't manufacturers just get the bloody car right first time around?

I'm not suggesting for a moment that Karl Benz should have realised, as he was cranking over his Motorwagen, that what he should have been doing was designing something like the C-Class and then shoehorning a 6.3-litre V8 into it. I'm talking about the way a given model supposedly 'evolves' over its lifetime.

There are countless examples of what I mean – probably as many as there are cars – but the general pattern of things goes like this. A new car is launched, and it's reasonable for us, the buyers, to assume that it's finished and as good as it can be, and that the people who designed it kept their noses pressed to the grindstone until no further opportunity for refinement of the idea could be conceived. But then, a year or two later, the maker announces that it has retuned the engine for increased low-range torque, and we in the motoring press become terribly excited about how much easier motorway overtaking has become.

Or perhaps the specification of the springs and dampers is changed to improve the ride and handling, so we all have a drive, talk to a suspension engineer for a bit and come away amazed at what they can do these days.

Or maybe some more welding points are added to the body

shell to enhance rigidity, and that's very welcome, and all part of the process of continuous improvement we've heard so much about.

But maybe a salient question is in order here, such as; why didn't you just do it like that in the first place?

It's not as if automotive engineering is a black art any more. It's a minutely understood and completely quantified science. No one with the brains to calculate that a car should run on 15-inch wheels could possibly fail to realise that it would work better on 16-inch ones, or that 180lb ft of torque is more useful if it's available at 2000rpm rather than 2500.Yet we are expected to believe that they miraculously work all this out only after 500,000 cars have been built.

A case particularly close to my heart is that of the Porsche Boxster. Two years ago, having realised that nobody fancied me any more, I decided that it was about time I owned a mid-sized two-seat roadster, and set about trying them all out to see which I liked best. Eventually, I settled on the Boxster 3.2S, for its combination of quality, driving dynamics, performance and discreet styling. It was clearly the best of the bunch, and I couldn't really fault it – beyond the rather churlish criticism that the engine was only 3.2 litres and not, say, 3.4, like it would be in the forthcoming Cayman.

A year or so later, Porsche boldly announced the 3.4S Boxster. They had shaved a little bit of metal from inside the cylinders or minutely altered the dimensions of the crankshaft and made the engine a bit more powerful. Excellent. But did they honestly expect me to accept that this was the fruit of a year's worth of scratching their egg-shaped heads and staring at a cutaway drawing of a flat-six? They must have known it was possible all along, in which case I'm forced to conclude that they deliberately sold me a car slightly less good than it could have been, and that the new and improved Boxster S was merely the one they should have given me in the first place.

Now at this point business types – the sort of people who,

at airports, pull their cabin luggage along on wheels and understand all those meaningless advertisements for the services of management consultants and the benefits of relocating to Wales – will be wanting to tell me that this is all part of keeping the market buoyant and managing customer expectations, or some such twaddle. It was once explained to me that Jaguar deliberately staggered the facelifting of its cars so that it would have something new to announce every year. But how can a car maker honestly plan a facelift? If they know the car can be made better, they should make it that way from the outset and stop wasting everyone's time and money. It would be like Gustave Eiffel designing the perfect tower but then building his first draft, just so he could return a decade later and make it look better; or a concert pianist recording a few bum notes so he could release a better version of the same CD later on.

The whole thing is a plot, obviously; the deliberate subversion of excellence in the interest of manipulating our desires and aspirations. Pah.

By the way, this column isn't quite as good as it could be. I deliberately wrote it that way so I can do it again next month, only better.

Is there a doctor in the garage?

Over the years, my local doctor has cured me of a number of minor ailments ranging from specific disorders of the bowels brought on by foreign travel to more obscure complaints such as general malaise. The only thing that has defeated her so far is my well-documented but largely unacknowledged tropical disease, which has yet to be formally recognised by medical science.

I quite like a visit to the doctor. She's a bit of a car fan, and as well as her daily driver she owns a 1980s 911 and, like most intelligent and interested people, she has a general understanding of how the thing works. But I'm pretty sure she's never picked up a spanner.

This brings me to an idea I've had for an experiment. I need a basically sound car suffering from some sort of typical but indeterminate engine malfunction, and a bloke racked with the ague but not in any way in a critical condition. A slightly poorly car and a person feeling a bit out of sorts. Then I want to give the car to a GP and the patient to a mechanic from a mainstream car business, and see who comes up with the correct diagnosis.

My money's on the doctor. And here's why. Medical training equips doctors, even non-specialists like GPs, with a scientific and analytical approach to identifying problems. Whatever training it is that car mechanics have doesn't do this. Car mechanics generally seem to guess, and just keep on replacing bits until the problem goes away, if at all.

I think the car mechanic business is facing some sort of crisis, and the problem has been generated, to some extent, by the cars themselves. A car is no longer a complex machine of many parts; it's now a collection of relatively simple machines bolted together. Sub-assemblies are invariably sealed, like those computer printers with 'no user serviceable parts inside'. If there's a problem with battery charging, they'll replace the whole alternator. And then the battery itself. And then perhaps the ECU computer and eventually the loom, or it might be the ignition switch. This wouldn't work in medicine. You'd go into the consultation room with a runny nose and come out with a face transplant.

Many dealerships, I suspect, aren't really interested in mending things at all. They're in the business of routine servicing, which I reckon has turned into an elaborate form of insurance. While your new car is under warranty, it will be honoured provided you stick to the service schedule and hand over the cash. The servicing is really simple stuff like oil changing and brake-pad replacement. Try taking a 10-year-old car with an unknown fault to a mainstream dealer, and watch them quake with terror.

As many experts will tell you, once the warranty is out you're better off with an independent, but even then you're not safe. Let's consider my good mate Colin, who has bought an old Mercedes which, obviously, went wrong within days. The man from his breakdown organisation said it was the fuel pump. The man from the local garage said it was a valve in the injection system. Someone else said it was an air leak. Eventually his wife suggested, correctly as it turned out, that there was so little fuel in the tank it wasn't getting through consistently. But imagine if he'd listened to them instead of her. He'd almost have a new engine by now when all he needed was a tenner's worth of unleaded.

Another example of this concerns my little aeroplane, the tailwheel of which went wonky so it would only steer to the right when on the ground. The sensible solution would be to pay a man to sort it out, especially as it's quite important. But hang on. The usual posse of pilots and amateur spannermen crowded round to say it needed packing with grease, that the links to the rudder pedal were too short, although they might be too long, that the retaining bolt was too tight/too loose/the wrong type, that the wheel was the wrong size. It was all bollocks, and at the end of the day visitors were still wondering why James May spent so much time taxiing around the airfield perimeter instead of just parking. I was doing this for the very reason that you would take a circuitous route from your house to the shops if your car would only turn in one direction.

See what I mean? The culture of spannering has somehow not encouraged a logical approach to analysing the problem, with the result that there are socket sets whirling around all over the country taking things apart unnecessarily and a huge business in place selling spares that aren't actually needed. And I know it worries people; people with classic cars, youths with ratty Peugeots misfiring on one, old dears with a Volvo they've had since new but that now won't start properly. What the hell are these people supposed to do?

Well, I've discovered that the best spannermen in Britain aren't actually in garages at all. They're at the National Motor Museum in Beaulieu. I was there the other day filming something for *Top Gear*, and while you may be familiar with the car collection itself, all shiny and beautifully laid out behind ropes, I am now in with the blokes in the workshop, who have to keep everything running.

Imagine what they're up against. There's over 100 years' worth of cars here, ranging from early Benzes and Renaults with ridiculous tiller steering to Grand Prix cars of the modern era. They can sort all of them, and often without the aid of off-the-shelf spares. Halfords simply do not have anything for a de Dion Bouton. The Beaulieu mechanics have to be able to mend the whole history of the motor car.

I mentioned to one of them a problem I was having with the carburettors on an old Honda motorcycle. He talked unassailable logic for about ten minutes in the manner of a scholar of Socrates, and eventually arrived at a component that I should remove, clean, and replace. I tried it when I got home and bugger me if he wasn't absolutely spot on.

There's a great business opportunity for Lord Montague here. Visit the National Motor Museum, and have your car fixed while you're there. I'm wondering if they can do anything about my cold sweats.

Trust me, I was a choirboy

There are ambitious dads everywhere who imagine that their sons will grow up to be better men if they play rugby, join the school officer cadet corps or volunteer for social work during the summer holidays.

And they probably will – up to a point. They may go on to manage banks, captain industry and generally uphold society with their yeomanlike qualities. We need people like this, so I wouldn't for a moment wish to discourage the accepted routes to the formation of good manly character. But if you want to be sure that the lad will mature into a truly redoubtable pillar of the male community, you need to put him in the church choir.

This is widely misunderstood. I hear people say things like 'Jenkins is a bloody good bloke. Winger for Chodford High you know', but this is no absolute guarantee of his dependability. If you're in a really tight spot and all hope seems to be lost, you want to be sharing the blood-spattered shell hole with a chap who once sang the solo in Samuel Sebastian Wesley's 'Blessed Be the God and Father'. He's your man.

I was a choirboy, and so were all the best people I know. It's why I turned out so well; that and being barred from watching ITV.

The choir – or, more specifically, the gaps between the weddings and other services – was the unforgiving arena in which we were made whole. Many were the couples who were eased into marital bliss at Whiston Parish Church with 'Jesu,

Joy of Man's Desiring' performed by a group of 13-year-old boys with black eyes, swollen lips, dead legs, Chinese burns and mental trauma. These were the result of severe and faintly occult rituals performed in the sanctity of the graveyard, which didn't do me any harm and went some way to making me what I am.

The only proper fight I ever had took place behind the teetering headstone of a woman who died when Victoria was a girl, was necessary to decide who would do the collection the following Saturday, and was with a boy called Kenneth, whose streaming nose remains as clear in my mind as the purity of his high Gs. And my shiner. I seem to remember that my dad gave me 50p for this performance, having recognised its significance in the formation of my character. I've no idea what happened to Kenneth in later life, but if you happen to be working with him today you can be assured that he is a man of unassailable moral fibre.

If you think choirboys are soft, you obviously never met any. You certainly didn't call our head boy a poof, otherwise you wouldn't have such a symmetrical face. As a choirboy, you were required to prove yourself; because, as a choirboy, you wore a dress.

So here comes the motoring connection, and unfortunately I've just realised it's a bit tenuous. I've been driving a BMW 530, which I think is a fine car and an interesting piece of modernist design. My criticism would usually be that it looks slightly knock-kneed. This particular one, however, was fitted with the M-Sport bodykit, which – perhaps uniquely in the history of bodykitting production cars – actually improves it. It makes the Five look very sculptural and contemporary.

But I had my reservations. Just as the cassock left me wide open to accusations of being a bit of a girl, the M-Sport BMW could be seen as a car in an aftermarket paddock jacket and might make me look a bit of a plonker. I would therefore end up driving it aggressively and discourteously just to redress the balance. As it transpired, though, I drove it like Jesus, because I was conscious that other people would assume I was a bit of a berk and was keen to prove them wrong.

I should have realised this. Occasionally I find myself driving the Range Rover we use as a *Top Gear* filming car, and because I know many people out there view a big 4x4 with utter disdain and are assuming poor moral rectitude on my part as a result, I drive like a man who's just collected a Ming vase. Put me back in the Panda and I drive like an idiot.

So if you're a fundamentally decent sort of cove – a reformed chorister, for example – do BMW, Mitsubishi, Subaru and Lamborghini a favour. Drive a rugger-bugger's sort of car. You can be relied upon to do it properly.

There you go. I told you this didn't stand up very well.

The seed of despair

I have pretty straightforward views on the business of saving fuel. Saving fuel is for fools. I don't even accept that, for some people, driving is a necessary evil, and that it should be done as cheaply as possible. Driving is not necessary at all, because trains and buses are very good these days and still cheaper in real terms. So kindly use them, and free up more road space for people like me who actually enjoy cars.

And as cars are my hobby, I can't really object to having to spend money on petrol, rather in the way that fishermen can't really object to having to buy maggots, and enthusiasts of hotel television can't reasonably object to the price of Kleenex. Given the choice between a car I'd enjoy driving and one that would save me £10, I'd always spend the extra tenner.

I even have an environmental argument in favour of thirsty cars. Everyone tells me that burning fossil fuels is a bad thing, and that it is destroying lives. In which case, surely it makes sense to buy something like an old Bentley or 60s American Muscle car and do your bit to help rid the world of this stuff. That way it won't be around to blight the lives of your grandchildren.

However, I've now changed my mind. I've changed it so much that I've sold my ageing Range Rover and bought a new 1.2-litre Fiat Panda, a car that steadfastly refuses to drop below 40mpg even if I thrash it and which, if I'm not paying attention, will readily crack 50. It saves petrol, and that's something we need to do.

We need to save petrol because the nation is in great peril. The nation is in great peril because of enthusiasm for alternative fuels. And amongst alternative fuels the most fashionable is biodiesel.

I don't like biodiesel; 'tis a silly fuel. For a start, it smells all wrong. The other day we were filming *Top Gear* near a farm where the stuff is made, and at one point the farmer went off to the bank in his biofuel-powered old Volvo. The sensation was similar to that experienced on driving past a kebab shop, only now the kebab shop seemed to be driving past me. That's confusing to an olfactory system conditioned over many decades. It's like Pavlov ringing his little bell then kicking his dog up the arse.

Unfortunately, biodiesel also smells pretty bad long before it makes it to the exhaust pipe. If I've understood *The Archers* correctly, it is made from oilseed rape, which stinks to high heaven just growing in a field. It's also an ugly yellow colour and is completely ruining the countryside, which, after all, is for driving through and admiring. England is supposed to be a green and pleasant land. I haven't given permission for it to be turned into a yellow hell that whiffs of Richard Hammond's unpleasant hair products.

It's a much bigger problem than you may have realised, driving around at ground level. I also fly light aircraft, and generally at fairly low altitude since I'm scared of heights. From 2500 feet I can see quite vividly just how much of the sceptred isle is being given over to this unutterably crap crop, and believe me it's quite a lot. The only possible benefit I can conceive of is that soon I'll finally be able to find my way back to the airfield, because it will be the only bit of the whole country that's still green.

Oilseed rape is absolutely and without question completely changing the face of our land, and for the worse. All of a sudden, the immutable Arcadian splendour that for centuries has been celebrated by our poets, artists and musicians, and which is at the heart of the rural idyll for which we all secretly yearn, looks as though it's been splattered with the sort of margarine they use in my local cafe.

Is this what we want? Do we want a hilltop view of Kent or Cumbria to look like the rejected artwork for an old Beatles album? I don't, so I'm doing my bit with a small car with a small engine that will help keep us in proper petrol for decades.

In any case, I've always liked small, simple cars with a sense of humour. The Panda is one such; immediate, efficacious, more than enough car without actually being much of one at all. It's surprisingly practical, amusing to drive and comedic in appearance. Oh, and economical, too.

Because I'm weak, I allowed the salesman to talk me out of the most basic model I'd vowed to buy and into the posh Eleganza version. But this means I have a trip computer and, at the touch of a button, can see immediately how well I'm doing in my quest to preserve what it was the poet John Clare was talking about.

You might think economy driving is boring. It is if you're simply trying to save money. But imagine the thrill that suffuses me when I see on the little dashboard display that I've saved another few acres of our island home from the yellow peril. This is something I can enjoy every day, unlike putting in a good time around Castle Combe.

There's only one problem: people have completely misinterpreted my motives. Some neighbours have imagined that I'm concerned about the difficulty in parking where I live. Others have assumed I'm taking advantage of the lower road tax for small cars. Couldn't care less. Someone even suggested that I'd caved in to public pressure about the unsuitability of big 4x4s in cities, and that I'd exchanged the old Rangey for a biffabout to ease my conscience. Not interested.

And then, the other day, I turned up at a *Top Gear* shoot

with the other two. Clarkson was driving the V8 Audi Q7, Hammond the Honda S2000, and I was in my Panda. 'Oh,' said a bystander. 'I'm pleased to see that one of you drives an eco-friendly car.'

How dare he? I don't give a stuff about the eco. Or parking, or congestion, or road tax, or fuel duty, or my carbon footprint. Me and my Panda are engaged in something far more important.

We're saving England.

Cheese grater, plug, wheel. It's obvious

One of the few things that Jeremy Clarkson and I agree about is that the world, overall, is getting better. Traditionally, everyone over the age of forty-five believes that the place is going to hell in a handcart, but if you think about this, it can't be true. Presumably people have been saying as much since William the Conqueror arrived, and if it were actually happening we'd have got there long ago.

In truth, everything improves. Life expectancy lengthens, standards of living rise overall, more diseases are banished and people in Manchester no longer have to eat coal. I can't imagine a single aspect of plague and jester-ridden medieval life that would have been better than the one we enjoy today.

Certainly, every artefact of man's making gets better. The car certainly does, but so do things that have been with us for centuries, such as the mechanisms of wristwatches, cement and woodworking tools. Very few things have reached the peak of their development and stayed there.

But there are one or two. One that springs to mind is the mouli cheese grater, a device that allows single men to make welsh rarebit without the ends of their own fingers in it. I've studied mine very carefully and can't see how it could be improved. Better materials would make no difference, and its dimensions and simple mechanism seem to have been perfectly refined. I've had mine for twenty years and the one you buy today is exactly the same. Mouli grater – sorted.

Another is the rubber bathroom-sink plug. The French popularised the type that is shaped like a metal mushroom and operated by a lever on the tap assembly, but they never fit properly and let all the water out. My downstairs guest bathroom has a sort of silvery disc that pivots in its hole, and I knew when I bought the sink that it would leak like a government ministry. It does, and I'm often awakened early in the morning by the stream of blasphemy emanating from the half-shaved faces of visitors.

It's all very well trying to express your 'design literacy' through your choice of bathroom fittings, but sooner or later you're going to have to admit that only a rubber bung on the end of a chain is truly reliable, and stick with it. We've known it for several hundred years. Sink plug – job done.

And now to the steering wheel. As a means of steering a car, I really don't think it can be beaten. Early cars had tiller arrangements, like boats, and I believe there may have been attempts to steer them with the feet, but the steering wheel had been adopted by Benz before 1900 and even British Leyland couldn't improve on it, although they tried with that quartic nonsense.

Elsewhere, and more recently, joystick control has been tried. Saab famously came up with such a system, and it worked at an academic level, but not so well that they let anyone drive it on a real road. More recently, it has been possible to engineer in feedback with elaborate sensors and microprocessors, but what's the point? Perfect feedback can already be achieved by joining a circular wheel to the steering mechanism with solid pieces of metal, so why remove that and then try to replicate it?

The steering wheel is a perfectly logical, truly analogue triumph for the man/machine interface, and I don't believe it will ever be usurped so long as the car is with us. Steering wheel – rock on.

Imagine my dismay when I learned that some people in the

automotive engineering community now believe that cars in the future will be steered with two thumb-operated buttons, in the style of the Playboy gaming console. If, like me, you've ever wasted any of your life away on one of these things, you will know this is a stupid idea. Opposed thumbs may be what separate us from the beasts of the field, but they were not meant for steering cars.

What worries me, though, is that the first car I ever drove was a real one, on a real road. Now, however, a new generation of drivers is emerging; one that learned to drive through virtual Britain on a Gamestation. Is it possible that thumb-steer for them is as intuitive as a wheel is for me? That the steering wheel only makes sense because that's how I was nurtured? That a wheel-guided car might seem as preposterous to them as a buttock-operated Mouli grater would to me?

I don't believe it, not for a minute. But I've just realised something. By the time you read this I'll be forty-five, and the world will be going to hell in a handcart.

I'll see you there. I'll be the bloke in the small Fiat with the funny circular thing in it.

When you have finished reading, you may hang up

The following very important piece of information is intended for all those friends and colleagues of mine who insist on talking to me on integrated car telephone systems.

It is now time for us to gird our loins, brace ourselves, and admit that these things – like the Soda Stream machine, buttoneer and toasted sandwich maker before them – number among those devices that endure for a while on the back of our fervent belief that they will be useful but in reality DO NOT BLOODY WELL WORK.

Consider the latest Mercedes E-class. I believe there was some disquiet surrounding the integrated telephone arrangement in the Command system of this car, because by the time it was launched the type of blue-toothed telephone solution required for its correct operation was no longer available. I gather that some owners are pretty sore about this, but they needn't be. It wouldn't have worked anyway.

I've had it up to here with people pretending to talk to me on built-in car phones. Jeremy Clarkson, for example, who remains convinced that every other telephone in the world is malfunctioning and cannot accept that the one supposedly incorporated in his SLK is about as useful as a speed hump on an airfield runway. I'm straining so hard to hear him that soon those minute bones in my ear, the ones that receive sound waves, will be on the outside of my head.

Only the other day, he rang me from the car and said, I think, that he had something very important to ask me. Whatever it was, I probably agreed to it. I have conducted whole conversations with him during which I've responded generically with 'yes', 'gosh' and 'ha ha ha' when he might have said something amusing, but in reality I haven't heard from the bloke in ages.

Not to be outdone, my other colleague, Richard Hammond, has had something similar fitted to his Porsche. Whenever he rings me, bored, on a car journey, I tell him to speak up because I can't hear him properly. He then regales me with an anecdote that would no doubt be quite entertaining delivered in measured tones in the warm confines of a local pub, but which loses something in a declamatory presentation style that conjures up an image of him turning more purple in the face as he bawls his way to the punchline. It's like listening to Windsor Davies read Psalm 23 in his *Ain't Half Hot* voice.

One day, out of interest, we spent a good half an hour scouring the cabin of the Porsche in search of the exact location of the little microphone that must be in there somewhere. It was nowhere to be found. The next time he rang, I realised we'd made a mistake in assuming it was *inside* the car. It's clearly up the exhaust pipe or inside one of the cylinders.

There's more. An important executive I know, the head of a very go-ahead company, often rings me from his car. The other day, he may have offered me some very lucrative work. Sadly, I'll never know.

What is to be done? Tricky. One friend found a way around the whole phones-in-cars law simply by Sellotaping his existing mobile to the centre of the steering wheel. I can hear him perfectly well, but now I have to shout to bridge the yawning three-foot chasm between the tinny earpiece and his actual ear.

And, as we know, one cannot use one of those wireless ear attachment things because one will end up looking like a bodyguard, someone in the early throes of elephantiasis or, worst of all, a plain berk.

The answer, I believe, is to return to those long earpieces-on-a-string that everyone was using a few years ago. These work and they're legal, but unfortunately they reintroduce another phobia of mine – crinkly wires.

Crinkly wires are hideous and everywhere these days: on computers, on satnavs, on home cinema systems, and on the 101 little plug-in transformers we need for recharging rechargeable things. They're the ruin of England.

So what I propose is a normal mobile phone with a long wire that retracts into its body at the press of a button, like one of those extending leads that people with very small dogs have. I've mentioned it to a nice man who works for the Carphone Warehouse.

And we know how successful my inventions are.

Citroën Ooh La La

A problem I'm feeling more acutely than ever these days is that there's a whole band of the motoring spectrum (sorry, been talking to some marketing people) that leaves me completely cold.

Luxury cars I've always loved: Rollers, Bentleys, old Cadillacs, anything unashamedly indulgent. I like supercars for their comedy value and true sports cars for the pleasures to be had at the man/machine interface. I've also had a lifelong love of truly simple small stuff – my peerless Panda, an original Mini, even the likes of the Perodua Kelisa.

But that leaves a lot of cars in the middle, and this is where I have some difficulty. I simply don't know what to make of a small MPV or lifestyle 4x4 soft-roader. The Vauxhall Zafira is clearly quite clever and the Toyota Rav4 is doubtless a pretty good car, but neither of them blows my frock up in any way. Same goes for a mid-size estate or a popular family hatch remodelled as a coupe cabrio with a metal folding roof.

Worst of all, though, is the spectre of the so-called executive car. I have to be truly honest here – I'm bored to death with Audi, BMW and Mercedes saloons. They are po-faced and humourless, even when they come with big engines and more knobs than the Radio 1 mixing desk. I can't drive an Audi A6 or 5 series without thinking I'm involved in something blue-chip and solutions-driven through the use of enabling technologies. I'm convinced that the people who drive these things use the word 'logistics' a lot.

I have therefore become a champion of the Citroën C6, which I have just driven to France and back with my new chum Oz 'Alka-Seltzer' Clarke, who was the bloke on the *Food and Drink* show back in the days when the television was a very large wooden box with a very small screen in the middle. So intrinsically 'right' was the combination of alternative French car and evidently British driver that I made it on and off the ferry and into Calais without a passport. I even made it back without having to pass a Britishness Test, although they did take me to one side to check the boot for Albanians. Maybe they'd heard how big it is.

At this point, I could easily slip into the usual drivel that accompanies any analysis of what is generally considered one of the most perilous purchases available to motoring man, i.e. a big French car. This would include a quote from Roland Barthes (a big fan of the original DS); something about intellectualism, cafe society, cheese, revolutionary tendencies, égalité and so on. What I really like about the big Citroën, though, is that it's so adamantly unfashionable. Here is a car that has never even heard of the Nürburgring. It flops into corners, and over a gentle undulation it performs a trick that only an old Rolls-Royce Corniche can match; that of appearing to remain suspended in space for a second or so before sinking back to earth. This, the shape of the rear window and the funky 70s-style door bins pretty much sell the whole car to me.

I can see that it's not perfect. The ride would be even better if Citroën had not fallen foul of the vogue for large wheels with low-profile tyres. A luxury car should have it the other way around, so that the tyres alone can absorb small ridges without bothering the whole suspension. My mum understands this perfectly well. The head-up display, which presents a digital speed reading apparently floating above the road somewhere in front of the car, is spoiled under certain light conditions, when the surround of the dash-mounted projector is also reflected in the screen. It's like that moment at an illusionist's theatre show when the mirror is inadvertently revealed behind a curtain.

And there are little things. The boot lid makes a rather insubstantial French noise when it shuts and, as has been true of every big Citroën since 1955, the engine doesn't seem quite big enough. The interior is also a bit conventional for a true Citroën: things such as the indicators and the ventilation controls are exactly where you'd expect them to be, whereas on a CX finding these things could provide a lifetime of on-road amusement.

But it's still great, a proper French barge that farts in the general direction of anything to do with handling or responsiveness. Better still, it managed something that my old XJ-S, even over a whole month of driving around France with the woody high-notes bloke, could never quite do for me.

Deep into a seemingly interminable monologue about the meaning of 'terroir' and the cigar-box scents of the velvety 1990 Bordeaux he'd just bought, the C6 – mercifully – sent him to sleep.

A postcard from France, part II

Dear readers,

Still having a super time here in France. The old XJ-S is going well, save for a small oil leak which I have traced – while firmly believing old cars to have a sense of irony – to the oil pressure sender unit at the back of the engine block.

This wouldn't be so bad on any other car, and would qualify as a running roadside repair at a small local garage. However, this is France, where all small local garages are characterised by being shut, and it's a V12 Jaguar, on which the oil pressure sender unit is about as accessible as the Queen's bedroom. The impression, upon looking under the bonnet, is that Jaguar's engineers placed the sender unit on a bench and then built the rest of the car around it.

None of this means anything to Oz 'hmm, fruit' Clarke, who can't believe that modern cars don't have carburettors and don't need to be decoked every winter. His only contribution to solving the problem is to observe that the smell of fresh 20/50 semi-synthetic landing on a hot exhaust pipe featured in one of his tasting notes for the 1988 Bordeaux Chateau La-La Land. We're talking here of a man who refers to the alloy wheels on his BMW as 'hub caps'.

It's quite refreshing to have travelled 1600 miles so far with a man who knows so little about cars, and whom I can bore to blazes with trivia about, for example, why the Citroën 2CV and VW Beetle are so different, despite being conceived around the same time in neighbouring countries and for essentially the same purpose; that is, mobilising The People. Well, he did ask.

In my opinion it was all about national ambition. The 2CV was designed to be capable of driving across a ploughed field, allegedly without breaking a basket of eggs placed on the passenger's seat. It was a true peasant's car, the product of a fiercely rural economy, designed to be repaired by people with access to little more than a brick and a piece of string. The engine was ruthlessly simplified, and the body- work came off so it could be beaten back into shape after witless rustics, half cut on the evil grog they still brew in sheds around here, drove into each other.

But the Beetle, while still a car for the Volk, was conceived by the Führer for the new *Autobahnen*, and especially the dead-straight one he envisaged running from Berlin to Moscow. Like most German machinery of the 1930s, it made the transformation to military equipment suspiciously easily. The Beetle formed the basis of the Kubelwagen and the Schwimwagen, in the way that Dornier's so-called 'fast mail planes' became curiously effective bombers.

This is the sort of thing I'm using to bore Oz Clarke to sleep in the passenger seat, thus preventing him from talking about the woody high notes and the long herbal finish. The flipside is that if I've had a drink and he's driving, I have to attempt to grab forty winks while he points to some desperate-looking rock-strewn vineyard and says something like 'Look at the terrain. You'll be able to taste the struggle of the vines and the wind from the hills in the 1995 Comtesse de Bomburg.'

The fact is that we're both nerds, but enthusiasts are always good company even if their subject is largely impene- trable. There's always common ground, too, and ours came in a drive across the Corbières Mountains.

The west side of the range is bad for vines. The rainfall is high, the soil is too fertile and has too much clay in it. It's heavily forested. Vines like harsh climates and poor ground; even the Romans knew that 'The vine shall not go where the wheat can grow'.

But we both agreed that it would be great in an old Mini. The road is very narrow, little more than a tarred track, and twists hideously. Huge power would be an irrelevance. A Mini would skip, goatlike, from bump to bump, and rasp on the short straights between the blind bends. The Jaguar was wasted on it.

The east side is completely different. It takes more heat from the sun, and the wind blows harder. It's much drier, and the ground is rockier. The vine strives for nourishment and gives us the aggressive red Carignan, Grenache and Syrah grapes, renowned for their heat and high notes of herbs and spices (says Oz).

And now the road is broader, more modern, and features longer straights between bends that sweep rather than twist, and where one can give it the grapes in complete safety. It's evolved that way to serve the hardy vintner in his van, but would also make the ideal accompaniment to a Porsche 911 3.2 Carrera like mine, or the one Oz once owned.

And that, we decided, was a good enough reason for drinking the local Fitou.

Dogs should be able to buy their own biscuits

I've always believed that animals are much cleverer than they let on; that sheep, for example, are actually great philosophers. What else can they be doing all day? They only stand in the road in Derbyshire so we don't realise.

Consider dogs. Dog owners are always inordinately proud if the pooch can open a door or recognise the sound of its master's voice down the megaphone of an old record player, but will not admit that most things apart from a simple stick-fetching or postman-biting stunt is beyond the witless beast.

However, I reckon that's what dogs want us to think. Occasionally, a dog accidentally reveals just how intelligent it really is. When I was a small boy we had one that, of its own volition, would go and collect my big sister from school, and even knew when it was the weekend and not to bother.

In fact, it could be that dogs are canny enough to realise that if the true extent of their capabilities become known, they will have to find jobs, open bank accounts and stand around the office water dispenser discussing the value of their kennels. What dog in its right mind would actually want that? As a dog you merely have to lift a paw to earn a good square meal, and as long as you fool humans into believing you're stupid you can continue to headbutt them in the crotch for a laugh, and get away with it.

This brings me to the subject of robotic cars. The idea has been around at least since I was a lad, when it was imagined that cars would run around autonomously, guided by networks of wires hidden in the road. I seem to remember VW experimenting with just such a system. Now, of course, the whole business is much easier. Satnav can know a car's exact position in time and space, and the type of sensor that allegedly allows the Lexus LS430 to park itself can be used to detect and avoid unexpected obstacles. The self-driving car is a technical reality, and as much has recently been demonstrated in California, where a competition to design a robotic car saw the winning entry cover sixty miles in an urban environment without hitting anything. But now we arrive at a problem.

Until the robot car can somehow be programmed to pick up the paper from the newsagents, it's a bit of a red herring. There is no pleasure to be gained from sending the car off for a nice drive on its own. For a while I might be amazed at the way it disappears out of sight down the road and then returns later in the day unscathed, but no more than I am when Fusker the cat does it (who, in any case, spends most of his time in the local pub pretending to sleep on a chair when really he's working on the libretto for his new opera).

This brings me back to dogs. Dogs can already fetch the newspaper and have been doing so, at least in the *Beano*, for generations. The dog could be sent off in the robotic car to pick up the *Telegraph* and other basic provisions, so long as you provide it with a list for the shopkeeper.

But perhaps we could be a bit more ambitious about this. I reckon dogs would like driving. The animal lobby will now dismiss this as cruel and immoral, but hang on a minute. Is it any worse than making a dog work for its living on a farm or at the gate of a scrapyard? It would certainly be more rewarding for the poor mutts. Furthermore, I've never met a dog that (who?) isn't a car enthusiast. Dogs bark at cars, chase cars, urinate on cars, like being in cars and like sticking their heads out of the windows of cars. It's only natural that dogs should want to learn to drive.

And I reckon they could do it. Spatial perception is very good in dogs. They can round up sheep, catch balls and jump over fences. Steering might be an issue, as they have no thumbs, but it must be possible, using modern electronics, to devise a steer-by-wire system based on head movement, so that the car simply goes where the dog looks. That, you're going to point out, will mean straight into a lamp-post or a lady dog. Again, that may just be what they want you to believe. Everything else – brakes, gearchange, starting, door handles – can be operated via pedals. Dogs have got four legs.

I'd like a dog that could drive for me. In fact it's time they did something useful instead of just sitting around in front of the fire all day and treating the place like a hotel.

Fido has had it easy for long enough.

The incredible disappearing road

I know you've all been waiting. So here, then, reproduced entirely without permission, is some official blurb concerning the government's *Manual for Streets*, which appears to be some sort of initiative aimed at improving the design of our, um, streets. Ready? Comfortable? Here we go.

> *The purpose of the* Manual for Streets *is to consolidate the necessary components for effective street design into a single integrated source of information and guidance that will facilitate professional communication and understanding.*

There's more!

> *The manual will recognise the full range of design criteria necessary for the delivery of multi-functional streets and ensure that practitioners have the most up to date information available on the considerations relevant to those criteria, including quantitative thresholds where appropriate.*

Now. Is it just me, or is this bollocks? Having already suffered the words 'facilitate' and 'delivery', I decided I'd rather kill myself than read any more about the *Manual for Streets*. But then I realised there hadn't been a 'solution' yet, so I decided not to kill myself and to make an effort instead. And I discovered some very disturbing things about the quest to make streets 'social places, not just traffic spaces'.

For a start, I'm always deeply suspicious of any attempt by the authorities to tell me how to enjoy myself. It's all a bit Strength Through Joy for my liking. It's a small step from here to morning exercise in the park and community singing, you mark my words.

But I do agree with the basic premise that streets should be social places. In fact, the street where I live already is one. People live on it, run in and out of each others' houses to borrow a cup of sugar, grow plants, talk rubbish, and moan about the bin men. We cook meals for each other, help each other with small DIY tasks and the subsequent rush to hospital, recommend builders and ask each other politely to turn the radio down. All this happens on my street. We even drive up and down it occasionally, although if other people drive up and down it too fast, we go out and shout at them. Multi-functional? We're already there, although we haven't yet used it as a landing strip.

How could this be improved? Well, apparently, speed humps could be removed – hoorah! – in favour of a doctrine of 'shared space'. But hang on. Surely they're not suggesting that there should be no delineation between the bit generally occupied by the cars and the bit that people walk on? My own experience of ignoring this well-established divide – when crossing the road, for example – suggests that this is a good way to get run over.

But I'm afraid that's exactly what they are suggesting. In the future, the road and the pavement will be on the same level, and trees will be planted at the edge of the road bit to 'slow cars down'. I don't think this will work. I was going to ring and ask Marc Bolan, but then I remembered that he died some time ago when his car hit a tree at the side of the road.

The authors of 'Manual' have been inspired by some

residential areas in places like Holland, where the street is essentially a children's playground and cars are slowed to walking pace and, at times, even excluded completely. This won't work in Britain, though, because our children won't play in the street. They're all too fat, apparently, from spending too long slumped on the sofa watching *Lazytown*.

Elsewhere, the *Manual for Streets* suggests the construction of something called 'pocket parks' – small grassy areas near roads to encourage socialising. Again, I'm not convinced. Roads tend to be noisy, and unless you're one of those mad French people who sits in a camping chair on the verge and watches cars all day, I don't think roadsides are very sociable places. There's a good reason why a mews house in London's West End is worth £4 million and one next to the A4 is generally boarded up.

More to the point, there's something a bit like a pocket park around the corner from my house; an area with benches and a cluster of trees. It is not used for socialising. It is used by tramps drinking Special Brew. We're all socialising in the pub, and won't give any money to the tramps because they'll only spend it on drink.

Admittedly, a lot of the thinking in the *Manual for Streets* is aimed at new streets; the streets that will need to be built around the hundreds of thousands of new houses that are needed to house all those people who are currently living in boxes. Or Latvia. But there is a perfectly good model for the successful development of new streets already in place in Britain – old streets. My own street was here for several hundred years before the car was invented, but seems to be able to accommodate it pretty well. The cars go down the bit in the middle, the people go along the bits at each side, and the bin lorry reverses into my wall. Simple.

Some of the thinking in the Manual just doesn't add up. One-way streets, for example, have fallen out of favour because, apparently, they 'encourage speeding, prolonging journey times'.

Exactly how going faster makes a journey take longer is not clear, but I'd be very interested to know, not least because it would render the life's work of Isaac Newton useless.

But here's where it turns sinister. From now on, T-junctions will be deliberately designed with sharp corners so that the approach to them will be blind. This will slow cars down.

I'm reminded of a project called something like 'Towns in Bloom' that ran when I first started driving. It encouraged, among other things, the planting of great beds of flowers in the central reservations of dual carriageways, especially at the point where they broadened on the approach to a roundabout. This looked great, but the roundabout was always hidden behind a huge wall of chlamydias. So you could slow right down and have a look first, or carry on at normal speed and hope to jink around circulating traffic at the last moment. The choice was congestion or death.

And now we have a similar plan to make junctions dangerous in the interests of road safety. The government will get you on a bicycle yet. Or kill you in the attempt.

What Audi could learn from Jesus

I know everyone is terribly excited about the new Audi R8, but every time I look at it I can't help thinking it's not quite right. It's all very well from the nose all the way to the rear edge of the doors, but then ... what is it? Too long? A bit too broad? Whatever it is, its makers have drawn attention to it by painting that bit of it black.

In fact, I know exactly what's gone wrong here, and by way of explanation I would like to turn to a figurine of Jesus that I recently acquired in an exchange of plastic novelty items with our saviour here on earth, Jeremy Clarkson. No point leaving the light of the world with that miserable sinner, because He'd end up in the back of a dark cupboard. I quite like having the old Nazarene around, so Jesus is currently brightening up a shelf in my kitchen.

Usually, my first reaction on considering this sort of thing is to conclude that Islam had the right idea in forbidding all depictions of the prophet Mohammed, thus saving its popular culture from a tidal wave of ecclesiastical tat. Consider the Mezquita in Cordoba, Andalucia; a great sprawling edifice that started life as a mosque but was later turned into a cathedral. The surviving mosque part is elegant, austere, dim, and altogether conducive to deeper thought. The church bit is gaudy to the point of revulsion, and includes a statue of the Virgin dressed as if preparing for an appearance in the popular celebrity trash mag *Halo!*.

But as Jesus nick-nacks go, mine's not that bad. He's dressed in a simple shift and sash, and shod with a pair of convincingly miniaturised Desert Dockers. His arms and legs are fully jointed, so he can be posed in attitudes ranging from the contemplative to the ecstatic. His torso incorporates a small electronic voicebox thing, so when you press a hidden button in the small of His back He delivers an uplifting Gospel quotation.

Never mind that, despite what William Blake told us, the Christ child seems to have spent some time on the east coast of America, or that he was miraculously conceived in China. Curious visitors to the May household will often pick up my Jesus, unwittingly press the voice button, and be reminded to love their neighbours. So Jesus of Hammersmith is fulfilling a useful civic function as well as a purely decorative one, and if I were the local Councillor Wonderful being interviewed on the radio, I could reasonably add 'in the community'.

Last night, Fusker the cat toppled the injection-moulded Prince of Peace from his position on a high shelf, causing his sacred head to come off, though without sustaining any permanent wounds. As I pushed it back into place, I noticed something odd. Jesus's head is a very different colour from Jesus's body.

Then I noticed something else odd. Jesus's body is blessed with most steroidally inflated pectorals and biceps ever to adorn a man who turned the other cheek. He didn't get those from helping Joseph in the carpentry shop, or just from overturning the odd money-lender's table. And what's with the gripping hands? They'd be great for holding, say, a machine gun, or for allowing Action Jesus to abseil down a rope, or even for helping him grasp the paddle of a miniature canoe. The only thing his hands aren't good for is being reformed into an attitude of prayer. They always spring back into the attitude of someone about to strangle the little children.

I know what's happened here. Someone who will not enter the kingdom of heaven has taken an existing action figure, substituted a vaguely Jesus-like head, incorporated a few out-of-copyright biblical passages and then dressed the whole thing in the garb of a poor Galilean in the hope that no one will notice. And then charged £35 for it. This is not an honest and heartfelt piece of Christian iconography at all. It's a Teenage Mutant Ninja Jesus, a craven image and, to my mind, blasphemous.

Here, then, is the problem with the Audi. I know they keep wittering on about how much they've modified the weight distribution, and I know it has a different engine, but in the end it's based on the Lamborghini Gallardo, which was designed as a Lamborghini Gallardo and looks better as one. I know platform sharing is supposed to be the saviour of car design, but this platform only seems to work in its original incarnation and won't tolerate a second coming. It just doesn't quite work.

You may as well try to pass a Camel Trophy Land Rover through the eye of a needle.

Maxing the Veyron – a piece of cake

You may have seen a short film on BBC 2's *Top Gear* in which it was my mission to verify Bugatti's claim that the maximum speed of its Veyron is a genuine 253mph.

And let me say straight away that it isn't. More careful calculation in the comfort of my office reveals that the 407kmh confirmed by the on-board telemetry actually equates to 252.9098mph. We knew that car makers lied about performance figures in the 60s and 70s, and we thought that sort of deceit was a thing of the past; but here we are in 2007, and even one of the world's most respected automotive operations can't resist adding a wantonly optimistic 0.0902mph to its latest car's top whack.

Still: it's quite quick, and ever since that day I've been seeking the one word that perfectly describes what it's like to drive a car at that sort of speed; at almost 100mph more than the agreed limited maximum for German super saloons. The disparity certainly feels greater than that, at least judging by the rate at which the armco and trackside trees sped past. It's a bit noisy, too, and the banking at the far end of Ehra's five-and-a-half-mile straight loomed very large very suddenly. When I looked, the needle was pointing at a number I've never seen on a car's speedo before. But despite all this, there is a word for it. And the word is: easy.

Sorry and all that. I could big it up and would probably get away with it. Only a select few have maxed a Veyron – the company keeps a record of their names in a little book, apparently – and no F1 car goes faster. There are but a few dozen people in the world who have been this fast in a car, so I could walk in to the pub and claim it as an act of heroism, safe in the knowledge that the next quickest bloke there would be the one who'd done 150 in his Fiesta diesel.

But, like him, I'd be lying. It's a piece of cake. You come off the banking, floor it, change up, and wait for the 'top speed' legend to appear in the dashboard display. The magnitude of the Bugatti engineers' achievement is not evinced by the absolutes of its performance figures, but by the impression that, at its top speed, the Veyron feels as though it's performing at two-thirds of its capabilities.

And yet – I don't believe I will ever go faster in a car. That there will ever be a faster car to go in is in some doubt. I know that aerodynamic drag is the issue, and that the drag increases as the square of the velocity. I also know that the power needed to overcome it is proportional to the drag times the velocity; i.e. the velocity cubed. I've therefore calculated, using amateur physics (and this is an open invitation to the usual assortment of engineers and science teachers to write in and correct me, with the aid of a graph), that merely to take the Veyron to 270mph will require an extra 215bhp.

That someone might build a car engine with 1215bhp, reliable enough to be used around town as well as at 270mph, is not inconceivable. But where am I going to drive this thing? There are some straight sections of *Autobahn* longer than Ehra's 5.5 miles, but they're rarely deserted. The 100-mile straight running across Australia's Nullarbor Plain sounds promising, but a stray kangaroo struck at 270mph is going to assume the solidity of Uluru. In any case, last time I was there the local rozzers got pretty shirty with me for doing 90.

No, I really do believe we've peaked with the Veyron. I know we said that about the rash of 200mph supercars that emerged in the early 90s, but this is different. The global road map simply will not admit of a higher speed, so that's the end of that.

And it troubles me. I've driven other cars at or close to their maximum speeds, and it's always been deliciously disconcerting. The Bentley Continental Flying Spur felt commendably stable at 190, but I can't pretend I was completely relaxed. The 1991 911 RS seemed to confirm the bar-room belief that any air-cooled Porsche was designed to kill you the instant you lowered your guard, and at an indicated 110 in my 1967 Triumph Vitesse the driver's door fell off.

But here is Bugatti, with its tiresome devotion to engineering excellence, ensuring that the highest speed I will ever attain on land will also be remembered as the least dramatic. They dumped me in the rarefied environment of 252.9098mph and left me wondering if I should put the radio on.

Bloody Germans. They always have to spoil everything.

The double-ended sword of motoring progress

I accept that my push-me-pull-you double-headed Alfa Romeo cum Saab interior themed limousine is still in need of some development work, but I don't think it should yet be dismissed quite so readily as it has been by some.

If you weren't watching, this was yet another *Top Gear* project vehicle, this time in response to a challenge to each make our own stretched car. It hadn't escaped our notice that every other one we'd seen was based around something predictably American, usually a Lincoln or, in cases of extreme chavity, a Hummer. This is all very well if you really are on a hen party, but it means the stretch limo can never be elevated to a more dignified role. Tony Blair couldn't, for example, use one to travel to an international summit, because everyone would expect him to climb out wearing no knickers and covered in ladysick.

No, for the stretch limo to become acceptable, it would have to spring from something more modest and European. So Hammond bought an MG-F, Clarkson found an old Fiat Panda, and I bought two cars – a Saab 9000 and an Alfa Romeo 164, both with 3.0-litre V6 engines. Nowhere in the British Constitution does it state that the two ends of a limo have to come from the same car.

Once I'd sawn the back off both, I also realised that there was no law stating that the limo must have a bonnet at one end and a boot at t'other. So I had some blokes weld the Alfa and Saab back to back to create the beast with two fronts. It's

not a completely new idea: diesel and electric railway loco-
motives have always been like this, and at their advent this
attribute of double-endedness was seen as a great leap forwards.
In both directions.

The advantages of this layout are so manifold I can't believe
no one's thought of it before. Delivering your client to the end
of a narrow street? Wave goodbye to limo-manoeuvring misery
by simply climbing into the other end and reversing out
forwards.

So far, limo drivers have been forced to avoid the narrow
Victorian streets of cities such as Manchester and London, but
not in the Salfa Romeab. On approaching a tight corner, simply
ask your passenger or a member of the public to climb into
the end you're not in and turn the wheel the opposite way. This
car[s] has a tighter turning circle than my Porsche, although
the Porsche doesn't sideswipe unsuspecting newspaper vendors
and orange sellers from the pavement.

Similarly, by turning the other steering wheel in the same
direction, the Salfa can be made to crab around obstacles such
as parked vans. Honda championed this type of four-wheel
steering years ago, but never really went far enough. The rear
wheels only swivelled by a few degrees, and they entrusted the
control of them to a witless computer. A man who has just
walked out of a newsagents does a much better job.

Admittedly, there are one or two administrative problems.
Insurance is difficult, because this is technically two cars. The
engine is a 6.0-litre W12 with a bit of a gap in the middle. Try
explaining this to a call centre in Karachi and expecting them
to quote you happy.

Furthermore, since the tax disc must be displayed in the
windscreen and must denote the make of car, and as this car
has two windscreens and two identities, it must be taxed twice.
But there are savings to make elsewhere.

Confronted with an illegally parked Salfa Romeab, the
warden must declare on the ticket what type of car it is. If he

concludes that it's a Saab, I can contest the fine on the basis that I have an Alfa, and vice versa. A policeman who asks 'is this your car sir?' will be compelled to state which car he's talking about. It doesn't matter which he chooses, because I can simply claim to be in the other one.

Best of all, though, is that this radical car is the perfect foil to the London congestion charge and all the other similar schemes under consideration. For the purposes of gaining type approval, the car is a Saab. Legally, the Saab is the front and the Alfa is the back. So it is registered as a Saab, wears the Saab's number at both ends, and appears on DVLA records as a Saab. But I can drive it into London without paying a penny. The automated charging system will show that a Saab 9000 has entered the congestion zone without buying a ticket, but when the photographic evidence is checked, Ken Livingstone will see only an Alfa Romeo reversing into the city.

I'll see him in court.

Mercedes-Benz forever

One of the few things motoring journalists can't tell you about a new car is how well made it is. Obviously, we can rattle on about the noise the door makes when it shuts, and lament excess shininess on the dashboard plastics, but none of this will tell you how well the thing will be hanging together in ten years' time.

On re-reading launch reports of the Triumph Stag, for example (no, really), I find nothing to say that this car will be prone to overheating and cylinder-head gasket failure. More recently, I didn't spot in my detailed examination of the then-new Alfa 156 that the minor electrical connections weren't up to much. And no one realised that the Peugeot 205 GTi would snap its cam belts and consume its own engine if you were unlucky. It was left to owners to discover this sort of thing the hard way.

The only way to tell how well a car was mantled in the first place is to dismantle it again, and the only person to have done this with any regularity was the man whose name shall be called manual, i.e. John Haynes. For the rest of us, turning up at a swanky car-launch venue with a trolley jack, two axle stands and a 99-piece socket set tends to arouse suspicion.

Still, about twenty years too late, I have just disassembled a substantial part of a 1985 Mercedes W123, the E-class before the one before the last one. People who mend old cars have told me before that this Mercedes was one of the best-built cars in history. It harks from a time when Mercedes avowedly over-engineered everything, when the customer paid a premium for that and was rewarded with a monastic interior and wind-up windows. You bought one of these Mercs if you enjoyed the nagging suspicion that everything, including the bits you couldn't see, had been done properly.

I can now confirm that it was. Taking the old E-class apart was a lengthy and baffling exercise, because there was always another hidden bolt, another screw, another fiendishly recalci-trant clip. The glovebox lid, for example, would not yield even to Jeremy Clarkson and his Cotswolds Screwdriver*; it would come off only by reversing the process by which it was attached in the first place. In isolation, it seems like an unnecessarily complex one, but time has proved it to be unbelievably fit for purpose.

So yes, the W123 E-class was a superbly well-made artefact on a par with some cathedrals, and it has got me thinking. I now know what old people are on about when they lament the passing of the mendable appliance. This week I have been forced by manufacturing timidity into discarding a kettle, a toaster, and a pair of binoculars. The kettle leaked, the toaster suffered a simple internal electrical failure, and the binoculars had water in them, but as none of them had been built to be rebuilt one day there was nothing I could do about it. Dualit toasters and the Rowlett model I have bought, for all their knowing ponciness, are held together with self-tapping screws and other things that can be removed and replaced endlessly. Like the yard broom of two-heads-and-three-handles fame, they are infinitely repairable.

Because the Mercedes was built properly, it came apart prop-erly. And because it came apart properly, it would go back together again. No doubt in the twenty-two years that my example had roamed the earth quite a few parts had been

---

*Hammer

replaced – it certainly didn't have its original gearbox, and various small components were obviously of newer vintage. But somebody once told me that only half of Westminster Abbey is the original building. So what? It's still Westminster Abbey. Whoever engineered my Mercedes must have wanted it to last for a very long time.

This is, I suspect, an increasingly unfashionable approach to making anything in large volumes. Sooner or later, and as with the kettle, the toaster, the laser printer and the washing machine, the car, even a superbly made one, crashes headlong into the argument about economic viability. But why? We drive around in a car for maybe ten or fifteen years, then decide we're bored with it or it's somehow not worth maintaining any more. So we throw it away – the whole car!

But look at the life of a typical W123 Mercedes like mine. It enjoyed what we would think of as a full life in the west before starting a new one as a taxi in the developing world, after which it began yet another existence in the hands of a private owner with the odometer already indicating a trip to the moon.

There is no reason why it shouldn't last until the end of time.

One good thing came out of the 1970s

I don't know if Santa has kept my letter dated December 1977, but if he has, he'll be distressed to know that I haven't changed my mind.

I was terribly grateful for the Airfix Avro Lancaster and the Top Trumps supercars pack, and I could even summon up a wry grin at the efforts of some misguided relation to help spur me through adolescence with a bottle of Boots Satinwood after-shave (I still have it, unopened). But these were a sorry substitute for that thing the mere thought of which was keeping me awake until dawn.

I was just a perfectly normal teenage boy in 1977; by day gazing wistfully out of the window during 'Naming of Parts', by night driven to dementia by unsated lust. All I wanted was to get my leg over the Yamaha FS1-E sports moped.

Surely you remember the Yammy Fizzie? The Fizzie was the world's best example of marketing opportunism in the face of a legislative loophole. The minimum legal age for a proper motorcycle was 17, but for years the British had been fitting small clip-on auxiliary petrol engines to conventional bicycles. My dad did this. Eventually, the fashion was framed by legislation that said a moped – the word is a contraction of MOtor-assisted PEDal-cycle – could be ridden at 16 provided it retained its pedals and the engine capacity was under 50cc.

And there it might all have ended, with history recording the ultimate expression of the moped as the French Velosolex or the similar machine, made by Raleigh, whose name now eludes me. At best it was a step-through such as the Motobecane or Puch Maxi. But right at the point when the rulebook was dusty with neglect, the Japanese motorcycle giants, plus a few Italians, recognised that they could snare their prospective customer base a full year earlier simply by building a high-performance 50cc bike and taking the expedient step of equipping it with nominal pedals.

This may not sound like much of a sales initiative by modern standards, but put yourself in the mindset of a 16-year-old, to whom the year that must pass before a car or proper motor-bike can be acquired stretches ahead like some hideous vision of eternity. The only acceptable escape from the drudgery of the bus and bicycle was the sports moped. Honda and Suzuki were at it, plus Garelli and even, I think, Moto Guzzi.

But the Fizzie was the one. Occasionally purple but usually yellow, its name in the teenage vernacular was derived from the phonetic implication of the legend on its side panel and invoked perfectly the character of the thing, even if it was a poor onomatopoeia for the exhaust note, which was more like rin-bin-bin. Owning the Yamaha was the ultimate and all-consuming desire of every right-minded coeval of mine. My mate Simon reported in some detail on a pioneering carnal encounter with a girl called Julie in a quiet bus shelter, but no one was impressed by that. Fischer's dad had bought him a Fizzie.

Obviously, I never had one. I honestly think my mother would have preferred to see me playing with a used hypodermic than riding what was, when all was said and done, a motorbike. Even the ultimate authorities eventually realised the folly of allowing 16-year-olds to own these things, and in 1978 the legislation was changed to restrict them to a top speed of 30mph. Ironically, the requirement for pedals was dropped.

Today, almost thirty years later, and since my mum wasn't looking, I finally rode a Fizzie. On the downside, it will only really do about 45mph, and not the 60 widely claimed. But here's what truly amazed me. It harks from the era of watch straps wider than the watch itself, of nylon paddock jackets, Barclay James Harvest albums, high heels for men, Old Spice and Liebfraumilch, all of which is the landfill of an earlier life. But not the FS1-E.

In fact, it is the first exception I have encountered to my own self-imposed rule that says you should never meet your heroes or revisit an old desire. I already know that the Lamborghini Countach was better as a poster than as an actual car. It's possible that Brian Cant and Derek Griffiths are just a pair of old bores. *Starsky & Hutch* is not half as good as it seemed at the time, the Muppets aren't actually funny and the same Julie who reduced my mate to ruins in the bus shelter is now probably a mother of three with a subscription to *Heat* magazine. The Fizzie, though, with just 49cc and 4.8bhp, turns out to be as exhilarating as I always imagined it must be.

And, in case anyone out there can help, I still want one really badly.

Out of date and out of mind

As far as I can tell, absolutely everyone in motoring journalism, the *Top Gear* production office, the motor trade, internet car chatrooms and down on the street is raving about the new Fiat Panda 100hp.

If you haven't seen it yet, it's a bit like a normal Fiat Panda only with a 1.4-litre engine, fatter wheels and a bit of light bodykit. I, and I alone, think it's pointless. I haven't actually driven it but I'm absolutely certain it's a waste of money.

To understand my dissent we need to take a look at the television; more specifically, at my television. Whenever I become embroiled in one of those lengthy discussions about consumer electronics I tell everyone that I, too, have one of those fatscreen TVs, and hope they're not really listening. Once the boasting starts I announce, calm as you like, that it's a 32-inch model, but without letting on that I'm referring to its depth.

Thing is, I bought a new television recently – by which I mean within the last ten years – and, subconsciously, I think that's it. I have my television set, and I can relax in the knowledge that I will never have to go through the appalling inconvenience of going out to buy another one. I also bought a radio for the home once. It was so long ago that pretty much every part of it except the valves is made of wood.

That was long before I bought the computer on which I'm writing this column but, to be honest, that wasn't in this century either. I hear that the 'podcast' is becoming a popular medium for the dissemination of news and opinion; even Mazda cars does them now, and there is currently one on the web from its UK marketing director in which he discusses the hot hatch sector. Unfortunately, expecting an iPod to connect with this machine is a bit like expecting Alexander Graham Bell's telephone to take pictures. In any case, most web pages come out as Egyptian these days.

I could go on. I shall. A while back the brushes on the electric motor of my washing machine wore out, so I summoned Hotpoint service. The earnest young man who arrived at my house – an obvious aficionado of domestic labour-saving devices – was utterly dumbstruck at what he saw. He was like an AA man who had been called out to a routine home start and discovered that someone was still using Tim Birkin's blower Bentley as day-to-day transport. 'Good grief,' he said. 'You must have had this since the 80s.' I didn't like to tell him I'd inherited it in the late 70s.

Back to the Panda 100hp. Regular readers may remember that I bought a Fiat Panda recently, the 1.2-litre version with 65 hp. I paid for and collected it almost exactly 24 hours before the new 100hp model was announced. And I admit I was a bit annoyed. It was a bit like buying a replacement round-pin plug for the kettle and coming home to find a man fitting the new square-pin socket to the kitchen wall.

And yes, I suppose I am the bloke who would have bought the Betamax video player, the Super 8 camera, the Sta-prest trousers and the Audi 80 with the radical Procon 10 safety system, the one thing that would stop me hitting my face on the steering wheel in the event of an accident.

Or it could be that I'm a bit tight, and that some vestige of a Presbyterian ethic leaves me reluctant to replace outdated possessions that, when all's said and done, still serve me perfectly well, even if they don't feature surround sound, MP3 compatibility, a built-in water purifier, digital reception, Wi-Fi, energy-saving bulbs or indeed 100 hp. The relationship I have with my personal appliances appears to be the one an 85-year-old has with a Honda Accord. Make do and mend, if it ain't broke don't fix it, it'll see me out, etc etc etc.

But there's another way of looking at this. Is there any reason why I should be tormented by the extra 35 horses Fiat is dangling in front of me? Should it worry me more than that my fridge isn't chilling my milk in a totally contemporary way? For a brief moment my 65hp Panda shone brightly as the latest thing. But now there's a superior model, it can simply function as my biffabout city car for decades of escalating obsolescence, just as my record deck does. This has improved it immensely.

There is a lesson for life here, one that right-minded people have known for centuries: choose once, and choose well.

Even if you choose badly.

Rubbish in, rubbish out

I think it was Trevor Baylis, the clockwork radio bloke, who said in a lecture a year or two back that Britain had become 'a nation of shopaholics who had lost sight of the value of production.' And it struck me that he could be right, so I immediately set about becoming an inventor as well.

My track record on this is not good. After almost ten years, I have finally given up trying to persuade the high-street banks to install cash machines with a 'gamble' function. Seems like a brilliant idea to me. Why worry about building supercasinos when normal people can throw away hundreds of pounds en route to the shops? You enter your PIN, ask for, say, £100, and then you have the option to gamble it. You end up with either £200 or sod all, but your account is still debited by the original amount.

But no one likes this, or my theoretical design for a domestic machine that recycles old copies of *Telegraph* Motoring into lavatory paper, thus cutting out Andrex, its delivery infrastructure and the annoying puppy, and thereby allowing you to cut your CO_2 emissions while reading about cars on the khazi. So I've moved on.

My latest thinking concerns shaving. If you're like me – and I know a lot of men are – you will cover your face evenly with foam and then shave it off in such a way that you can see what you might look like with a Hitler tache or Emerson Fittipaldi's bugger-grips. But the effect is always slightly unconvincing.

So what's needed is a range of coloured shaving foams – black, several shades of brown, blond, grey and of course not forgetting older people who were born before being ginger was eradicated. Carrot-tops always look good with beards, and they will see just how like a wizard from a Harry Potter film they could look by using May's 'I can't believe it's not stubble' shave stick.

I've written to Gillette and have so far received no reply. Their objection, I suspect, is that encouraging beard growth has a direct impact on razor sales. They needn't worry. No man in his right mind actually *wants* a beard; we just want a laugh pretending to have one for a few minutes before breakfast. It's merely a novelty item, a passing *divertissement*, like Tiptronic gearboxes. But no.

So I've now applied my mind to motoring. First, and taking my inspiration from celebrity chefs' ranges of cookware and celebrity gardeners' branded trowels, I wrote to Shell suggesting that they market Jeremy Clarkson Unleaded. This would be exactly the same as normal unleaded but dispensed through a pump bearing an image of the great man's face and the legend 'poweeeeer' in big letters. It would make absolutely no difference whatsoever to the performance of your car but would cost 1p per litre more, in return for the warm glow of satisfaction you'd get from the implied advocacy of this towering colossus of tyre destruction.

Why not? As far as I can make out, the Nigella Lawson casserole dish is exactly the same as any other, and won't prevent my own casserole from turning out like anything other than hardcore. It's also ruddy expensive and yet the last time I went to John Lewis, it had sold out.

Here's a better one. Not really an invention at all, just an idea; and not really an original one at that, since Volvo tried it once but seems to have given up on it. I want someone at the British Standards Institute to establish a regulation-sized centre-console car bin and a regulation bin-bag to go in it.

I'm amazed this has never happened. My modest little house is full of bins. There are two bins in the kitchen, a bin in my office, bins in the garage, a bin in the yard for plant clippings, a bin in the bathroom and even a bin in the spare bedroom, so that when my mates stay over after dinner they have something to be sick in. There is a bag to suit each of these bins.

But there is no culture of in-car bins and bags, which is odd when you think of the steady ingress of rubbish headed the way of the typical runabout: American Hard Gum packets, parking tickets, scribbled directions, the leaflet a breakdown organisation gave you at the motorway services, tissues, the groaning partwork that passes for a VAT petrol receipt these days. Tons of the stuff. When I cleaned out my old Range Rover prior to selling it, I found one shoe and a small item of broken garden furniture.

Bins are what separate us from the beasts. You have them everywhere else, you should have one in the car. Apart from anything else, if you own a Mercedes S-class you'll finally have somewhere to put the owner's handbook.

A postcard from France, part III

Dear readers,

There's something that has bothered me ever since I arrived in France and started hanging around with Oz 'I'm getting raspberries' Clarke. And it's this.

In pretty much every arena of human activity, we unashamedly embrace science and its exploitation through industry. Even those who purport to be living on the set of *The Good Life* will marvel at how a DVD player can be bought for as little as £35, or wonder how civilisation ever developed before the mobile phone. Things that were once the fancies of sci-fi writers have become disposable trinkets, and all through the economics and efficacy of manufacturing science and mass production.

And this is a good thing. The world, I'm convinced, and despite what old people tell me, is always getting better. We have more aid to our labours, better means of communicating with our loved ones, less chance of catching beri-beri and more chance of being cured if we do. And all thanks to what an Italian fridge-maker used to call the appliance of science.

And yet ... when it comes to food and drink, we feel better if it's produced by bucolic peasants in smocks toiling in fields like an illustration from John Duc de Berry's book of hours. We think that to industrialise it is to spoil it, when clearly we believe the opposite of everything else. Why?

This week on my wine tour, for example, I was expected to stand barefoot in a wooden tub of Chardonnay grapes in order to crush them. This, I pointed out to the vintner, was a job that should be done by a machine, and ideally one made by Toyota. But no. The human foot, I was assured, is the best instrument yet devised for gently breaking the skins of the grapes and beginning the process of extracting the juice. What's more, it is the direct involvement of the rustic wine-maker – even if in this case it was me – that assures the character of the finished produce.

There's a lot of this sort of thing on our trip. The harvesting and selection of grapes by hand, the ploughing off a vineyard with a mule instead of a tractor, and some mystical nonsense about earth energy in the nurture of some Merlot crop. All of this gives wine a local flavour, apparently.

But what French wine doesn't offer, it seems, is any sort of consistency, and consistency is the key to modern consumerism. Henry Ford reduced costs by mass production, but before that Cadillac demonstrated that it was the inter-changeability of parts that made it possible. This, in any case, had already been demonstrated in the clockmaking and gunsmithing businesses. Even modern Japanese car factories, which produce cars in 'work cells' and have overthrown many of the old ideas of series production, owe their success to the utter fidelity of the parts they use. It is the art of manufacturing that ensures that a new brake calliper bought from a Ford spares operation will absolutely and unequivo-cally fit your Ford Focus.

Car industry bosses, at least on the quiet, would also admit that the exclusive hand-built car (of which there are very few true examples left anyway) is not really as depend-able as the mass-produced one. It may be rarer and trimmed with more exquisite materials, but it won't actually be as good. All other things being equal, manufacturing is superior to the craft tradition. So why isn't Renault making the wine?

Now I know why. The fact has been widely recorded and trumpeted by the wine fraternity, but the terrain and climate of a country like France really can change significantly within the span of half a mile. A slight increase in altitude, a shift in the composition of the soil, a subtly different geographical relationship to the path of the setting sun: these things really do make a difference. The earth is anything but consistent, so how can its produce be? Maybe the wine bores have a point.

But hang on. The earth may be cussed in Europe, but else-where in the world it is utterly uniform. In Australia, New Zealand, Chile and California, for example. There, the terrain is the same for miles on end, the sunshine and rainfall utterly predictable, and the wine business unencumbered by the bloody-mindedness of *Appellation Côntrolée*. And in these places wine is truly manufactured, and almost always to a higher standard than a humdrum French co-operative can manage at the same price.

So in the modern world, you're almost certainly better off drinking Chilean Cabernet and driving a Honda. But misty-eyed romantics needn't despair. The exclusive and very tasty 1988 Chateau Pichon Baron will be available for some time yet.

And I suppose you could always drive a Bristol.

The pointy end of motorcycle purchasing

In one sense, the British public has a moral obligation to pursue the sport of darts. The days when we were compelled to practise archery on the village green, so that we might be prepared to see off invaders, are long gone; yet darts, generally thought to have derived from all that bow-and-arrow stuff, is a convenient way of keeping the eye in, and with the Channel Tunnel the risk of an assault from France is, if anything, worse.

These days, though, the dartboard is generally used to settle debts or establish whose round it is. People have played the stock market with darts and I've seen debates over holiday destinations resolved with a bit of left-hand-nearest-the-bull malarkey. But what about a new motorcycle?

It all began with an everyday pub debate over etymology. What is the difference between a treble and a triple? Treble, we decided, and after several of them, means three times something, as in 'treble 20', i.e. sixty. Triple means three of, as in the three-cylinder Triumph Speed Triple. You can probably guess where this is going.

I've fancied a Speed Triple for a while. I've even managed to save up for one. But because I am wracked by Protestant self-loathing whenever I spend a large sum of money, I cannot bring it upon myself to simply buy a motorcycle. Especially as, when all's said and done, I already have one.

These things have to be earned, and it was decreed that I could have the Trumpet when I'd scored three treble 20s in one go. What's more, the triple treble top (see?) must be achieved during a regular game in which I might at times be obliged to aim for other numbers in order to maintain dignity in the face of my usual opponent, Tony.

Now he's a man who knows his arrows and likes a wee dram afore he throws. One day, when he has achieved true greatness, I shall be in a position to write his biography, a stirring tale of personal triumph over the debilitating effects of leglessness – *Reach for the Scotch*.

My personal darts peak arrives after about three pints, when suppleness returns to the wrist. So after an hour or so during which I was regularly rewarded with the evocative thud of mild steel penetrating the Edwardian oak panelling of the Cross Keys, I had settled into an impressive rhythm of scoring quite well.

In fact, I threw two treble 20s and the pub, had there been anyone else there, would have descended into an electrified silence as, for my third throw, I positioned my right toe against the ancient brass strip burnished and patinated by a million cheating feet. Legs braced, elbow tucked well in, eyes focused, muscles instructed to repeat the impulse that had launched the previous two darts, I released the flashing javelin of salvation.

In the pantheon of blunt things there are old Stanley-knife blades, neglected carving knives and rusty chisels. There is that tool that allegedly makes extra holes in belts and there was the school bandsaw. But the world does not admit of a point more dull than the tip of a dart kept in a jar behind the bar of a local pub. For complex geometric reasons such a dart is more likely to bounce off the thin wire that cruelly divides motorcycling satisfaction from despair, and so it did.

Now the rules (or at least the rules in my pub, and if you don't like them you can go elsewhere) state that if the point of the rebounding dart lands behind the oche, the throw may be taken again. And it might have done. Or it might not. It was difficult to tell, because it had gone behind the radiator.

It says something about the reputation of the place that the sight of two grown men lying facedown on the floor elicited not so much as a murmur from two regulars who chose that moment to enter through the normally hazardous side door next to the board. But once the gravity of the situation had been outlined to them, they, too, dropped without demur to the dusty boards and unanimously declared that I had earned a re-throw.

And so, having brushed the 100-year-old dead spiders from its mangled flights, I launched the dart of joy anew. I cannot deny that the onus was on me to check that the shaft was still firmly screwed to the body of the missile, and that it was because it wasn't that the two separated in flight and the point removed a huge wooden divot from the scoreboard while the tailpiece fluttered pathetically to earth.

As a famous darts commentator once said, there's only one word for that. And neither of them is 'magic'.

The case for cat-nav

Every now and then a piece of technology arrives to provide the long-awaited answer to a question that has troubled man ever since he descended from the trees. The radio telescope, for example, which helped to establish how old the universe is, and how big.

More recently, I believe some of the advances in driver navigational aids may now be in a position to resolve one of the great mysteries of the human condition, a conundrum that has baffled people for hundreds of generations and which has been vexing me this week in particular – namely, where the bloody hell is my cat?

Normally, I don't even want to know where Fusker is. I know that he is, like most cats, something of a community animal. I believe, in fact, that in some countries this fundamental characteristic of cats is recognised to the extent that is not legally possible to 'own' one.

He is a free spirit, a neighbourhood cavorter with the stature of a small loaf and the heart of a lion, hairy-hearted confirmation that, as I've always suspected, the animals are not really our friends. I know he's in and out of everyone's houses, and that he convenes with his cat chums on a garage roof in the afternoon to exchange notes on armchairs, radiators and who's roasting a chicken. For me, it's always been enough that, as night falls, he announces with the clunk of his catflap that it is to my home that he returns to fulfil his role, correctly identified by Woman, as a furry reminder of human neediness.

But now someone else is feeding him, and presumably with wild Scottish smoked salmon, because last night a portion of his favourite free-range Spam was left untouched in the cat bowl. He even turned his nose up at the meaty treats from Sainsbury's, and they seem to think he can taste the difference.

It's a problem because it's time for his tri-monthly worming medicine, which comes in tablet form and is crumbled into his dinner. This stuff is not found in the leftovers from my posh neighbours' Japanese puffer-fish takeaway. As he's not eating his proper food he's not getting his dosage and that's bad for him.

So I need to know where he's going, and there are a couple of ways of doing this. The other day, I met a former MI5 bloke who schooled me in the arts of video bugging. Tiny cameras, about the size of a lentil and connected to recorders not much bigger than a box of Swan Vestas, can be hidden almost anywhere – in a book, in a pot plant, in a wall clock. Amazingly, this stuff is available on the high street. He even had a video camera in the knot of a tie he'd bought from Spy Rack.

But while I could hide the camera in Fuzza's fur, I'd have difficulty disguising the recorder. I think he'd arouse suspicion wearing a rucksack. Then people would know they were being watched and wouldn't behave normally, in the same way that they're not honest when filling in the *Cosmopolitan* sex survey. Also, and like George Formby when he was cleaning windows, I might see something I'd rather not know about.

No: the answer, I believe, lies in the workings of my portable NavMan satnav device, which fits comfortably in the palm of my hand. But it's only that big because it has to incorporate the screen and the little speaker through which the digital harridan berates me. I'm betting that the electronic circuits that deal with the business of decoding the satellites' signals are minute, and would probably fit inside a cat collar.

Meanwhile, my desktop computer has something called a

Wi-Fi device that means it can communicate wirelessly with the box that connects me to the World Wide Web of Lies. The range of this thing must be about the same as the extent of Fusker's territory, since it seems to work in the pub sometimes.

So, incorporate the transmitter in the cat, and I'll be able to watch his movements on a moving map on my screen. Voilà – Cat Nav. Old dears worried about the whereabouts of Fluffy have wanted something like this since the Egyptians turned the cat into a deity. Get on to it, NavMan. There are millions of cats in Britain and no one knows where any of them are. You'll clean up.

And talking of cleaning up: if you're the one feeding my cat and you're reading this, then I hope he pukes right in the middle of your new sitting-room carpet on the day you have it laid. Like he did on mine.

Driving is easy, and that's just as well

For a while now, I've been wondering if cars would be more engaging if they were a lot harder to drive.

Of course, some people like to pretend that driving is a very specialised skill. The Institute of Advanced Motorists, for example, who sometimes seem to imagine that the rest of us have not grasped the enormity of the undertaking.

Then there are track-day driving instructors, who often sound like human resources executives, talking about personal development and building progressively on a skills base. I worry that even our own Stig would sound like this if he could talk, but since he's the result of an early experiment in bionics – his urine is just a stream of transistors – he can't, fortunately.

It would be nice to drive a car knowing that few other people were qualified to do so, but, as I have observed before, it's not like being an Apollo astronaut or a member of Pink Floyd. Everyone I know can do it and I must therefore conclude that it's easy.

By way of illustration, it's interesting to compare a journey in the car with a trip in the little tin 'n' rivets aeroplane I fly. When I walk out of the door to take a spin in the Fiat Panda, I don't even bother to check if the tyres are all inflated. If they're not, I'll know by the end of the road and I can stop and do something about it. But on the aeroplane, the tyre condition is just one of hundreds of things I'm supposed to consider before I even get in the thing. Brake lines as well. It's so complicated that I have to carry a little book reminding me of all the things I'm supposed to look at before I can go anywhere.

They include the hinges on all the control surfaces and the rods and wires linking them all together. I have to check all the lights, the fuel tanks, the fuel itself for moisture or contamination, the condition of the metal skin, the oil level, the brake-fluid level, the prop for nicks and chips, the engine cowlings for security, the functioning of the buzzer that warns of a stall and the heater for the pitot tube. I have to check that the belt driving the alternator is in place, since it's difficult to repair with a pair of tights in flight. I've never done that with a car.

By now it's time to climb aboard, alone, because Richard Hammond will have gone home in a fuming rage of impatience. But don't imagine you can just fire up the engine. You have to check for free movement of the throttle, mixture and carburettor heat levers, for full movement of the controls, that the heating and ventilation works, that all the circuit breakers are in place, that the instruments all work and that the clock is telling the correct time. Now, perhaps, we can put the key in.

But we still can't start the engine. First, it's necessary to turn the electrics on, including the fuel pump, and make sure that the warning lamps designed to indicate failure of some of the above will light up when needed. The engine may have to be primed. Then it's necessary to make sure that no one is standing next to the propeller. Then the starter can be cranked, assuming it's not already dark, in which case it's time to pack up again.

With the engine running, a quick check must be made of oil and fuel pressures, of the vacuum for the instruments, of the output of the alternator, that the twin magnetos that govern the engine's ignition are working properly and independently, and that the radio is on and correctly tuned. And now, finally, and what seems like half a day after I collected the key from the ops room, the aeroplane moves forward.

There are lots of things to check during the taxi to the runway. The brakes, more instruments, the setting for the altimeter, the nosewheel steering, the radio reception. Near the runway, it's necessary to make sure that the engine will run at full power, at idle power, on each set of magnetos, without an unacceptable drop in oil pressure, and without overcoming the brakes. The flaps have to be sorted out, the locks on the door have to be checked, and if Richard Hammond were still there I'd have to tell him how to get out in an emergency.

And now the kite rolls forward and at around 55 knots (slightly more if Hammond is aboard) and the rush of air over the wings, in accordance with the findings of Daniel Bernoulli, rewards us with the gift of flight. But it doesn't get any easier up there.

One instrument indicates the airspeed. But since the air varies, this will be different from the true airspeed. What's more, the aeroplane flies through the air as though it were still, but it might actually be moving across the land. So to go somewhere, I have to know the true airspeed and the wind speed and how this will affect deviation from a true heading calculated from a map but which has to be converted to a magnetic heading in order to use the compass, into which magnetic variation must be factored in order to arrive at a track and real speed across the ground itself. It's said that a good landing is one you walk away from, and a very good landing is one you walk away from leaving a serviceable aeroplane behind. In my view any landing made at the airfield I took off from is a bloody miracle.

And yet . . . I like all this stuff. I admit it makes me feel a bit clever, in the way that stockbrokers get a kick out of needing to know the time in New York and Tokyo. Wouldn't mundane car journeys be a lot more involving if there was a lot more to worry about?

To find out, I borrowed a 1922 Buick, to see what driving was like in an era when the motorist was still a minister to a rare and baffling machine, rather than the mere operator of an everyday device. The pedals were the wrong way round, and so were the gears. There was no synchromesh – no roof either, come to think of it – and there were levers on the wooden steering wheel to alter the fuel mixture and the ignition advance for hill climbing and 'fast' cruising. There was some sort of manual fuel pump, no indicators and a cranking handle for starting, which made stalling at the lights annoying for everyone.

And I absolutely hated it. It was far too difficult. After half an hour of driving around at 25mph I was utterly exhausted. This is why old people tend to take driving so seriously. They remember when it was a lifetime's work.

So, to return to my original question: would driving be more interesting if it was a bit more difficult? No. Sorry, I've wasted your time.

That North Pole nonsense

The fundamental problem with any journey to the North Pole is that there are, in fact, two of them: the magnetic North Pole, which is a physical phenomenon, and the true North Pole, which is a cartographical convention established from the shape of the earth and the axis of its rotation. Bored yet? This is only the beginning.

You might wonder why this is. Well, the magnetic North Pole is useful for most basic navigation as it determines the direction of a compass needle. Unfortunately, it moves around a bit over the years, and severely buggers up mapmaking.

Also, for the purposes of dividing the globe into lines of longitude, which relate to time as well as position, the true North Pole is better because it's right at what we think of as the 'top' of the planet. Serious maps are oriented towards true north, and if navigating with a magnetic compass, as most amateur sailors and airmen do, it is important to allow for something called 'magnetic variation'; that is, how many degrees away from true north your magnetic north is. This changes around the planet and is indicated on maps using something called 'isogonal lines'. In London, for example, magnetic variation is currently about 3 degrees west.

Bloody hell.

It's important to establish which North Pole you are talking about when using an expression such as 'let's go to the North Pole'. Technically, if you are at the North Pole, everything is to the south, no matter which way you turn. If you are at the magnetic North Pole, then the true North Pole is to the south, and if you are heading to the magnetic North Pole and find yourself at the true North Pole, the North Pole is still to the north. Unless, that is, you are working to true bearings, in which case you will stand at the true North Pole with your magnetic compass still pointing north, but actually that's south.

Anyway, we decided to head for the magnetic North Pole; or rather, Clarkson and Hammond did. Clarkson, the best off-road driver 'in the world', would go in a Toyota pick-up truck, and Hammond would eschew at least a century of progress and be towed there by some dogs. I didn't actually want to go at all. I hate snow, I hate extreme cold, I hate dressing up and I knew it would involve some camping, since there are no hotels.

But Jeremy insisted, saying I should come along as his navigator. This was pretty insulting really, because navigating to the magnetic North Pole is a simple matter of heading north with a compass, obviously. Even if, starting from Canada, I followed the wrong end of the needle I'd know about it once we got to Mexico.

Now we have completed this great odyssey, I can categorically confirm that going to the North Pole, by whatever means, is a completely futile and miserable exercise. It starts with the special Arctic clothing, all of which is covered in stupid zips that catch in everything and makes a really irritating and deafening rustling noise if you so much as scratch your head. Taking a poo in the Arctic involves removing ten layers of this stuff and then quite literally freezing your nuts off. And that's if you don't get eaten by a bear while your trolleys are down.

You might imagine that an endless vista of snow, interrupted only by the occasional abstract ice sculpture, is something quite beautiful to behold, and it is. For an hour or so. But after a few days it's a bit like looking at a screwed-up sheet of plain A4 paper. Open the freezer compartment of your fridge and look at that for two weeks to get an idea of what it's like.

The extreme cold – minus 30 at times – is a nuisance. Because the atmosphere is extremely dry up there, none of your personal effects ever freezes solid; they just become very cold. However, the instant you spill anything – your gin and tonic, say – then your trousers become part of the landscape. I took a packet of Johnson's baby wipes with me, for the purposes of 'washing', but within ten minutes they'd become a scented iceberg. Only in the Arctic have I been presented with the problem of having to keep my tins of tonic warm enough to drink. And don't imagine that we were nice and warm in the car – we weren't allowed to have the heating on because it would interfere with our special misery-spec Arctic onboard cameras.

I hardly dare remind myself of the camping. It's not just that the tent had to be erected and dismantled every day, or that the zips on that always stuck as well, or even that the rudimentary kerosene stove set light to my face. The real problem was having to share it with Clarkson, who was incapable of helping to put the thing up, even though the job required the use of nothing more than his favourite tool, a hammer.

I'm not a great camper but Clarkson is a worse one. Every night he would zip himself up completely in his cocoon-style sleeping bag, even his head, and then blaspheme into the thick down all night long. It was like sharing a tent with a big sweary maggot.

There was little respite during the day, whatever the day was. Because it was the summer, the sun simply cavorted up and down the sky like some cosmic fairground attraction, and at one point we had a huge row over whether it was lunchtime or midnight. We honestly didn't know. Driving was a simple matter of enduring the constant crashing and rattling of the overloaded Toyota, punctuated by the occasional dull report of another exploding tin of Schweppes as we crept further north (magnetic).

I honestly believe that it was only the drink that kept us going. Even asking Clarkson if he'd like some ice in his G&T

wasn't funny after a day or so. The conversation started well enough, with intelligent debate about politics and geography, but after a few days we were arguing for hours about the significance of just-in-time manufacturing versus the importance of interchangeability of parts, and by day four we had been reduced to food fantasies involving sandwich spread and sausages. I cheered Clarkson up with the caviar and quails' eggs I'd smuggled past the Arctic exploration Nazis, and he rewarded me by shooting my tin of Spam, for which I wish an especially virulent pox upon him still.

And when we finally arrived at the Pole, there was nothing. No monument, no visitors' centre, not even a cairn of ice cubes. It was just more snow. We intended to leave a small *Top Gear* flag we had made, but discovered that we'd forgotten to bring the stick for it.

With the mission accomplished, the doctor we'd taken along as part of our small support team asked me, 'So, James, now you've done it, do you think your life will be better or worse for the experience?'

I decided it would be worse. Because occasionally I would remember it.

A brief history of history

This week, I have been reading a book on the history of the Honda CB750 motorcycle. Very good it is, too. Did you know, for example, that the crankcases of the very early models were cast in sand, and that it was only once production was established that Honda moved over to more efficient die casting? Me neither, until now. Early bikes had painted fork stanchions, whereas later ones were chromed. There's a lot of this sort of thing in *Honda CB750* by Mark Haycock, published by Crowood Press.

I can also recommend *Mercedes SL Series* by Brian Laban (Crowood again). You may not know that much of the oily underpinnings of the original SL, regarded by many as the world's first true supercar, were borrowed from the rather dowdy Mercedes 300 saloon. I did know this, but only because I've read it before.

I like this sort of thing; very detailed analysis of a very particular artefact or event from our past, especially if it's a car, an aeroplane, or something to do with the Second World War. But at the same time, I worry about it. History, I mean. I worried about it at school, too, and all because there seemed to be so much of it.

History, at school, was somehow made interminably dull by a teacher who had some pet theory about enclosure in the Middle Ages and never talked about anything else. But I was dimly aware that there was also some stuff to do with Greeks,

Romans, Egyptians and the Battle of Britain. Later in life I discovered that history is actually fascinating, but at the same time I had to admit that there was even more of it than I first thought. The Aztecs, the Chinese, the Irish potato famine. It just goes on and on for ever, or will if we're not careful.

Civilisation is getting older, and at the same time more and more of our existence is being committed to record. There will come a time when the whole of history is too big to contemplate, and no one person will be able to construct even a sketchy notion of how the world came to be the way it is. Socrates, or Plato, or someone else who was idiotic enough to write things down instead of just keeping it to himself, said that he who will not learn from history is doomed to repeat it. How can we learn from it? It's too big.

This has all been brought home to me over the past few weeks, because I've been working on a BBC series about the history of technology in the twentieth century. Unfortunately, we have only six half-hour programmes in which to address this topic, and it isn't really enough; not when there are already several thousand carefully researched words in a book dealing with one car or motorbike. And the technological achievements of the period 1900–1999 is just one aspect of one century. It doesn't go anywhere near pre-industrial Japanese architecture or the development of Hinduism.

The twentieth century is especially significant to my concerns, because it revealed that the too-much-history menace is a bigger threat than we thought. Not only is history lengthening like a shadow with our forward march through time, it is also, in a sense, expanding backwards with new means of investigation. A lot of what we used to call pre-history – that is, from a time before any records were made – was in fact recorded perfectly well in things like carbon deposits or soil chemistry, which we can now read perfectly well. Now a couple of American physicists have measured the residual radiation from the first fraction of a second after the Big Bang, giving us an echo of the moment of creation itself. So history turns out to be a lot older than we first thought.

My conclusion from all this is that there will eventually have to be some sort of enormous natural catastrophe of the sort Noah experienced, just so the slate can be wiped clean and we can be saved from the tyranny of an incomprehensibly complex past. Double history was already an hour long in 1974. Imagine what it will be like in 4050.

And this brings me back to the car. Doom merchants, environmentalists and cod philosophers say its invention was a disaster, and that it will ruin the world. How can it? Its presence occupies the same time as the twinkling of a star in the true span of history, which, as we have seen, will end soon anyway.

And next time around, there's a good chance that Middle East politics, health and safety or Ralph Nader will be invented first, in which case it will never be allowed anyway.

Bring on the flood.

Give me a car, not a cuddly toy

There are several reasons why I could never feel entirely comfortable driving a G-Wiz, even if I managed to overlook the rule of life that says a gentleman does not drive a plastic car.

Firstly, it's a battery-powered electric job, and I've never been able to drive such a thing without constantly worrying about what will happen if I run out of juice. It's all very well claiming that it does the equivalent of 600 miles per gallon, or arguing that all petrol stations should offer a few three-pin sockets, but the fact remains that it has a range of only forty miles or so and takes at least six hours to recharge. Six hours is a long time, even compared with that brief glimpse of eternity that is the age taken to fill up my old Bentley, and with the best will in the world there isn't six hours' worth of entertainment to be had at the Happy Bean coffee stop.

Because it's electric, it's green. But is it? How do you know where the electricity has come from? Has it come from a windmill in George Monbiot's garden, or a power station fuelled with old tractor tyres? The other day Sainsbury's offered to sell me some electricity, and some of their vegetables come from Israel.

But never mind any of that. What would bother me above everything else is that it's a bit cute. Why? Why can't it just look like a car?

I realise that if you're designing a truly small car, some

aspects of legislation, and the simple fact that people don't become smaller while they're driving, would make it difficult to style it on the lines of the Lamborghini Gallardo. The lights have to be a certain height above the road, which means they may have to stick up a bit. There's a limit to how low the roof can be, so a short car will end up being disproportionately tall. But this is no excuse for making the Smart fortwo look like two frogs mating.

Cuteness in small cars is a very disturbing trend. I've heard psychologists talk of something called the 'Bambi Effect', which explains the way nature makes the offspring of all intelligent mammals very attractive, so that their parents will feel more inclined to look after them. This seems to work very well for babies and kittens, but driving around in Bambi is taking it a bit far. It's also rather unmanly.

Some cars that are more oochy-coochy-coo than they perhaps needed to be include the Smart, the Nissan Micra, the Toyota Aygo and its relatives, the Daewoo Matiz and the Ford Ka. Now we have the Mitsubishi iCar. I haven't driven it yet but it would appear to be quite well thought out. But did the headlights really need to be that doey? Does it really need a half-witted smile and those chubby cheeks to work? One suspects not.

To my eye, too much cuteness makes a small car look as though it's apologising for even trying to be one in the first place. Cute small cars make me think of those dull grey-suited executives who wear comedy ties because, hey, they're dead funny really. A cute small car seems to say, look, I know I'm just small and a bit pathetic, but look at my face! How could you not love it?! That would be like kicking a puppy!

Not only can this be rather embarrassing, it also perpetrates the notion that small cars are essentially rubbish. A cute small car is a bit like someone who begins an anecdote by saying 'It was really funny . . .', which means it wasn't. Tommy Cooper never said that, and no one ever imagined that the Rolls-Royce Phantom should be in any way a proper sweetie.

This is where we're going wrong. Not only can small cars be perfectly good as cars per se, they can also be among the most entertaining you can lay hands on, and this much needs to be reaffirmed through the offices of sensible, adult styling. The only excuse that needs to be made for a small car is that you have one because you enjoy driving too much to tolerate a big one.

I say this because I've really fallen for my Panda; for its sense of urgency, its liveliness, the eager thrum of its piddling 1.2-litre engine, and the pure hilarity to be had from chucking it at a small roundabout. It doesn't offer the visceral thrill of the Porsche, but in many ways it serves up more cerebral pleasures, which in themselves attest to a more advanced state of the human condition.

It's a great car, and even better when you consider how easily Fiat could have ruined it. They could have lost their bottle and made it really adorable.

We are not amused

I've decided that I'm jolly glad I'm not the Queen of England. I think it must be really boring.

True, she's probably never had to open a curtain or wash her own smalls, but on the other hand, she can't slip down the Windsor Castle for a swift pint and a game of arrows, and though she may be heir to a throne that once seated the empress of India, she still can't sneak out for a crafty late bhuna with Phil at the drop of a crown.

Being the queen *and* a car enthusiast would be a right royal pain in the arse. When you're the queen, presumably the world's top car makers queue up with lavish gifts of bespoke motors. But you have to find a bloke in a hat to drive them for you, because once out on the road you're at work, and expected to sit in the back and wave at the plebs. The Rolls-Royce Phantom series, for example, is one of the world's most expensive and exclusive ranges of cars. The queen has owned a whole string of them but I doubt she has driven one, ever. Even I've driven a Phantom.

I know Aitch Em agrees with me on this one, because for many years she kept a Rover P5 saloon in the Palace mews purely for recreational driving. A while back, I rang up and asked if I could have a go. This, I thought, could go one of two ways. I could end up in the Tower with no head, or our sovereign might see fit to reward me for my loyalty with some small token of her appreciation. Cornwall, perhaps. After some harrumphing and long telephonic pauses while people walked very slowly up and down long corridors, the keeper of ye queen's key fob agreed to lend me the old girl for an hour. The Rover, I mean.

'Bloody hell,' I thought, as I selected drive and trundled away, 'I'm driving the Queen's car'. 'That's a nice old Rover,' said an elderly bloke through the open window. 'I'm afraid it's not actually mine,' I replied. 'It's the Queen's.' He began to back away with an alarmed expression like people do when confronted by a dangerous drunk. But it really was the Queen's car, not a trapping of state occasion. Somewhere (though not, sadly, in the glovebox, or I'd have nicked it) is a V5 registration document proclaiming the 1972 P5 to be a one-owner vehicle and the property of Elizabeth Windsor, a lady.

As one constantly torn between unswerving loyalty to the crown and outright support for a republic, I found my monarchic motoring experience quite persuasive. The editor of *Country Life* once proclaimed the Queen to be 'cool', and I think he's right. The P5 is a cool car to have if you could have any car in the world. David Beckham has a brand new Bentley, but he's only the king of football. The Queen's the Queen and has one of these, so I want one, too.

There's something very comforting about the royal Rover. It's original, unmolested, patinated with age and use and, I'd like to say, it smells faintly of the Royal We, but as that isn't actually true, and as relations between the media and the Palace are strained, I'd better not. I'm hoping that by now there is a little brass plaque on its dashboard, like the ones seen on those old Le Mans Bentleys, to proclaim that this particular P5 was driven by Her Majesty Queen Elizabeth II of England and her humble servant James May, who may be found at the sign of the Cross Keys, Hammersmithe.

But my new-found royalist tendencies took a few knocks on the journey. The first thing I noticed was the fuel gauge. There's more four-star in the tank of my Atco lawnmower, and I haven't lived anywhere with a lawn for fifteen years. You'd have thought that the Queen, of all people, would have been able to afford to put in a tenner's worth down at Tesco.

I also couldn't help noticing that there wasn't a valid tax disc. There wasn't an expired one, either; in fact, there wasn't even a tax disc holder. So I have to pay road tax to use the Queen's highway, but the Queen herself doesn't? I suppose she thinks she owns the road. As usual, there's one law for the Queen and another one for the rest of us.

Most disappointing, though, was this. In my own car, I keep a tin of those boiled travel sweets. On the lid is a little crest and the words 'By appointment to Her Majesty the Queen.' I've always understood this to mean that these are the sweets the Queen herself eats on the long haul up to Balmoral. That, in fact, is why I buy them.

But in the centre console of the Queen's car? Nothing.

A load of horse's arse

Regular readers will know of my uneasy relationship with the countryside; with its mud, darkness, terrible smells, unsociable-hours animal noises and strangely-dressed people making their own chutney.

Recently, I've spent quite a bit of time driving through the countryside (since that's what it's for) and there's a lot about it I like very much, especially in Britain. I like the way that, over the course of a mile or two, the widescreen vista can shift from wild rolling hill to swaying cornfield to stone-walled patchwork to verdant hedgerow and then to wooded glade, where a member of the public walking his dog is about to discover a body.

But there's a lot that has been baffling me for years, notably some of the signs. Now quite often you will see one at the end of a driveway saying something like FREE RAGNE EGG'S £2 1/2 DOZ, and I can see why that might draw the odd inner-city escapee in. No matter how fresh the eggs in your local supermarket, they will never offer quite the same fleeting fluffiness as those popped in the boiling pan while still warm from the cow.

The other day, though, I came across a piece of cardboard propped against the gate at the end of an enormously long driveway on which had been writ large, in crayon, POTATOES. At first I thought this was another invitation to buy, but how could it be? I don't believe anyone has ever driven through the countryside and been seized by a sudden craving for a potato. Potatoes are not a time-sensitive foodstuff. I can buy them from the newsagents where I live, they last for months in the bottom of the fridge and may even reproduce if I'm lucky. So what was this sign? A celebration of the fecundity of Arcadia? A boast? Or what?

What it really meant, I decided, was something like 'Potatoes. See? You come out here in your shoes and your fancy car, but you hadn't thought about potatoes, had you? And where did you think they came from, eh? Not from your feeble urban garden paved over to facilitate off-street parking, that's for sure. And don't you forget it'. It was a riposte, really; a way for our ever more-beleaguered bucolics to remind us townies that just because we're free to drive around the countryside, that doesn't mean we will ever truly 'understand' it. I also saw a sign that said MANURE. Same sort of thing. The obverse would be me erecting a sign outside my house saying ELECTRICITY or SEWERS.

I like this theory and I'm sticking with it, because it finally explains why horseboxes and horse lorries always have the legend HORSES painted across their tailgates. Every time I come up behind one I wonder what, exactly, my reaction should be to the news that there are horses in the vehicle in front, other than amazement that anyone should still be using such things. Why do I need to know?

People who display those tiresome 'Baby on Board' stickers can always argue – with some conviction, I suppose – that they are there to remind the emergency services, in the event of a sudden flood or multistorey car-park collapse, to rescue the infant that might otherwise go unnoticed on the back seat. But this is never going to be an issue with a horse, especially as any approach to a horsebox ultimately rewards you with a view of the beast's arse. So I wonder if this is just another example of the country folk trying to put us in our place.

Still, let's try being a bit more sympathetic here. There is a country code for drivers just as there is for walkers, and it may be worth reminding ourselves what it is. We should slow down for the village, so as not to alarm anyone deep in a reverie of walnut-pickling or corn-dolly manufacture. We should give a wide berth to cyclists and ramblers. We should not park in gateways or narrow lanes where we might impede the movements of tractors, and when encountering a horse actually being ridden on the road it is important to drop down a couple of cogs and get by as quickly as possible, thus minimising the animal's discomfiture.

And if you do find yourself behind a large vehicle transporting horses by road, there are some things you should definitely not do. Most importantly, never let a horse know that you are afraid. Do not discharge a handgun out of the driver's window, and never, ever dress up in the brightly-coloured dragon costume from a Chinese New Year celebration and dance around in the road.

Not that any of you were going to.

Porsche – taste the difference

Here's the scene. I'm in my Porsche, I've been driving through suburbia for some time, and I'm slightly bored. But then, as the houses peter out, I finally spot a good-looking stretch of derestricted A-road, and I think to myself, 'Wahey. This looks good. I think I'll put it in sport mode.' I press the button, the legend 'sport' appears on the little display in the rev counter, and off I jolly well go.

I should point out that this is the first car I have ever owned with a sport button, and I've been utterly delighted by it; by the thrill of being able to reconfigure my car to suit the driving environment, or whatever it would say in the owner's hand-book if I could be bothered to read it. But all of a sudden, I'm beginning to feel like a bit of a mug. After ten months, I've had to acknowledge that the sport button in the Porsche Boxster doesn't really do anything at all.

Now before all the Porsche bores write in, I do know that in sport mode the parameters of the traction control are relaxed so that the skilled driver can display his prowess by gathering up a whiff of incipient oversteer with an armful of opposite lock, or whatever it is men in pubs claim to be doing of a weekend. But nothing is of less interest to me. That's just something that happens in *Autocar* magazine.

But at the same time, the electronic brain that governs all this also sharpens up the throttle response, making the car more lively, more frisky, more responsive to the inputs of the dedicated helmsman. Or does it?

No. I've just done a simple experiment. I drove along a dual carriageway at a constant 60mph, throttle held precisely, and in sport mode. Then I turned sport mode off. The car faltered, and then carried on as normal at about 57mph. As far as I can make out, sport mode simply means slightly less pedal travel is required for the same result.

There's quite a lot of this sort of thing about; of products designed to be as good as possible and then downgraded slightly so that we, the consumers, can either press a button or pay a little extra money to have what we wanted in the first place. In the BMW M6, for example, the driver can twiddle the i-Drive control to select either 400bhp or the full 500bhp. But why, if you'd bought the M6, would you want 400bhp?

The Bentley Continental GT owner can twirl a similar knob to select the 'comfort' setting on the car's suspension. Why isn't it just like that anyway? Under what circumstance would you want a Bentley to be anything other than comfortable?

These things may give you a temporary warm feeling, a sense that car makers are considering their customers and allowing them to tailor a car to their individual requirements, but if you think about it a bit harder you'll soon realise that they are just wasting your time.

Elsewhere, a friend of mine has a vacuum cleaner with a button marked 'Turbo Power'. Press this, and full suction is delivered. But surely it's always required. No one wants to leave some of the dust on the carpet.

Now I think about it, I'm becoming suspicious of Sainsbury's Taste the Difference range. I've always bought Taste the Difference cheddar cheese – it's a little bit more expensive than the other stuff, but it's also a little bit nicer. Now, though, I'm wondering why they don't simply make all the cheese taste that good. I'm worried that they're deliberately producing mediocre cheese so I can go through the motions of selecting the good stuff.

What really bothers me about the sport button is the idea that, as a Porsche owner, I would somehow want to 'buy in' (as the marketing people would put it) to a little bit of extra sportiness. I 'bought in' to the notion of a sports car when I went in to the Porsche showroom and handed over a fat cheque for the Boxster instead of veering off to the Citroën garage and buying a C6.

In any case, we've got this the wrong way round. All of Sainsbury's cheese should be top notch, save for a small selection of leftover 1970s British Rail sandwich cheese, branded as the Taste the Awfulness range, there to remind us how much worse it could be.

And the Boxster should be built as a supreme sports car but fitted with a special button that makes the steering vague, the ride choppy, the handling floppy, the interior plastics too shiny, the engine less powerful but the fuel consumption worse.

This button should be marked 'America'.

A postcard from France, part IV

Dear readers,

By the time you read this, my French wine tour will be over. I will have crossed the silver sea (which serves it in the office of a wall, or, as a moat, defensive to a house etc) and returned to the sceptred isle.

And as I return early on a Saturday, I can already tell you exactly what I'll be doing. If it's between 9 and 11 in the morning, I'll be drinking several large mugs of builders' tea made with the one ingredient that the French, for all their talk of *terroir*, cannot readily provide; that is, fresh milk not ruined by the UHT process. I know it's a bit predictable for me to bang on about the inability of foreigners to knock up a cup of char, but let's not be soft about this. If the people of Somerset can make brie, the people of Lyon should be able to make tea. The town is almost named after a tea-room, after all.

From around 11 to about one in the afternoon, I'll be in the Ritz (not *that* Ritz – it's a cafe at the end of my road), after which I'm going to have a long lie down with my cat, during which I hope to shake off the terrible *'Allo 'Allo* accent I've accidentally acquired. By eight I'll be ready for dinner, which I imagine will be either cod and chips or a chicken tikka bhuna, after which I shall retire to the local pub and shut the lid on my holiday wine romance with several pints of Fullers. That lot should see me pretty much back to normal.

There are quite a few things I'm not going to miss about France. Oz Clarke's endless talk of the woody high notes; garlic, the devil's own vegetable; shops and indeed whole towns that are shut; camping; bread and jam for breakfast; French motorway sandwiches; and *manigance*. This is a new French word I've learned, meaning, I'm told, a combination of hanky-panky, jiggery-pokery and skulduggery. I'm not entirely sure what any of those things are individually and in English, so imagine how obstructive they are when combined in one Frenchman.

At the same time, there's a lot I *will* miss about this country. Some fine wines, to be honest; some magnificent Frenchmen, but especially the mechanic who rebuilt the Jag's exhaust after I tore it off on an old tank trap in the Alsace region. Given the history of the place, it's difficult to know which nation to blame for this. Amusing cheeses, chateaux, lovely D-roads, *babyfoot*, and the sort of ribaldry that can only develop between two blokes on a very long car journey.

And the Renault 4. The Citroën 2CV is perhaps more iconic, and more people would recognise one, but it is the Renault 4 that truly endures. The cardboard Citroën is becoming surprisingly rare these days, but the Renault is still everywhere. You cannot drive for more than an hour in France, and often only for ten minutes, without seeing a Renault 4 doing what it was meant to do, which is usually transporting a pig, or something like that. Spotting Renault 4s will never pall as an en-route *divertissement*.

The Renault 4, I suspect, is subject to *Appellation d'Origine côntrolée*. If it isn't, it certainly should be. The Renault 4, as the president himself once said, speaks volumes for France. It is more than a simple people's car, it is the wheeled totem of France's desire to retain so many of its peasantine traditions, it's rural bedrock. It is not a classic coveted by enthusiasts, as the Renault Dauphine or Citroën Big 6 is. It is merely an old car that refuses to give up.

Italy has a car like this in the original Fiat Cinquecento. They are still around in huge numbers, confirming the efficacy of the original simple design in their ability to keep going. Like the Renault 4 in France, they are not preserved relics. They are simply still current. People are driving Renault 4s and Fiat Cinquecentos because somehow, and in direct contravention of all logic, it still makes sense to.

I do not think that Britain has a car like this. We have the Morris Minor, the MkII Jaguar, the original Mini, and the MG Midget. Very British they certainly all are, but in very different ways. And they are now largely in the hands of devotees. There is not one single and ubiquitous car that feels like the product of some government initiative designed to reaffirm The British Way.

The Renault 4 is like that, a car that rumbles on in open defiance of the new world order, and in bloody-minded denial of everything that has happened since.

A bit like the French wine business, really.

The future of motor racing, and it's cheap

Every now and then, over at *Top Gear* TV, we have something called an 'ideas meeting'. I suppose other people would call it 'the pub', but as far as we're concerned we are confronting the white heat at the very kernel of creativity, and if industrial lager is needed to keep it at bay, so be it.

An ideas meeting involves everyone on the production team and anyone can, and does, contribute something, even me. The other day, I piped up with 'How about some classic motorsport?' Well, it went so quiet I could hear the producer's clothes rotting.

And I sort of understand why, really. In the phrase 'classic motorsport' I struggle to find a single word that would have caused us to break step in the delirious headlong rush to the discussion about the exploding caravan or the Stig-in-a-Zonda scene. And indeed we didn't.

Apart from anything else, motor racing, at any level, involves a lot of things I don't really approve of: dressing up, taking it seriously, being on time, and oversteer, which is nothing more than a leftwing plot. The beauty of the motor car is that it has liberated the common people and allowed them to stray far and wide, so the idea of using it to arrive at the point you started from two tenths of a second sooner than you did last time flies in the face of everything I hold dear about cars. The car is the most poignant instrument of progress the world has produced, so using it to go nowhere seems strangely ironic.

Even so, I can't believe that motor racing is as boring as it often is. Which is why I have come up with the 1275cc challenge. The producer obviously isn't interested and won't let us talk about it, so I'm going to do it here instead, since this is my column and he can't stop me.

It will take the form of a hillclimb – a hill in every country is pretty easy to find – and will be an international series with appropriate television coverage. As with all proper motor racing, there is a strict formula to keep the playing field reasonably level. But this time it does not hamper technical progress or imagination, it simply keeps it all at pocket-money prices. It's a vision of egalitarian motorsport, and first came to me while I was driving along in my Rolls-Royce.

The car must have been powered, when in production, by the 1275cc variant of the venerable A-series engine. It must retain this engine, and it must be road-legal, with an MoT. The two obvious contenders are the 1275 MG Midget and one of the later editions of the original Mini. Sound examples of these are available for £1500 or so and can also be enjoyed on the road when you're waiting, like Steve McQueen, between races. This ensures that the technical advances forged on the track will translate directly to the car you drive on the road, largely because it will be the same one.

Already, this strikes me as interesting. We have a low, light rear-drive car versus a short, upright front-drive one. For decades people have been arguing in pubs about which layout is best, so now we'll find out in the unforgiving arena of cheap competition against the clock. Hammond can be in the Midget, since he already has one, and I'll take the Mini, as I've owned several and still have the Haynes Manual. Providing the car fits in with the simple criteria mentioned above, anything goes.

Now we arrive at the great stumbling block of motor racing. Make the rules of the formula too vague, as I appear to have done here, and somebody very clever will find a way to gain an insuperable advantage with ground effect or traction control or something like that. The rules are then made ever tighter in the interests of maintaining a good viewing spectacle but the outcome is predictability and the stifling of inventive talent. So here's the clever bit.

The second part of the formula, and the only other rule, applies not to the car itself but to the team's toolbox. Only manually-operated hand tools can be used in the preparation and maintenance of the racing car, and electricity and compressed air are banned.

So you can do what you like, but you can only do it by hand. No one can re-bore the engine to 1500cc, because that requires a machine tool, which is not allowed. Similarly, it will be impossible to trim a few thou off the cylinder head to improve the 'squish', unless you're so brilliant you can do that sort of thing with a file. You can fit a turbo or bigger brake calipers, but only because you can do that with one of those all-in-one toolkits from Halfords.

There is even an incentive here to drive intelligently. Pit stops are obviously to be avoided, because without compressed air wheel-changing will become an interminably tiresome task involving wheelbraces and blisters.

You can widen the track and fit fatter wheels if you want, but if the car is to pass an MoT – which, remember, it must – it will then need bigger wheel arches. If you can't do this with a sheet metal bender and a pop rivet gun, you're stuffed. Excellent. This simple tool rule means a cash-strapped teenager in a lock-up is no worse off than a team entered by Williams.

Best of all, because electricity is banned under the formula, there can be no laptops and tiresome telemetry. That sort of thing is boring and more to the point expensive, which penalises the poor people. Here is a form of racing that rewards artisanal skill and resourcefulness rather than the big budget stemming from a corporate sponsorship deal. What could you possibly spend the money on anyway? More spanners and Nomex? It won't help you win.

I can't help thinking this is all rather brilliant. We're always looking for the future of motorsport. We've tried the MPV challenge and half-car racing, but neither of them quite caught on. This, I believe, will. It will be fun to take part in, fun to watch, instructional, educational and, most importantly, cheap as chips.

By my calculations, we could produce a new world champion for a total outlay of around £2000.

Cars are rubbish

Recently, a friend of mine gave me a vintage telephone as a gift. You know the sort of thing – one of those brightly-coloured 70s types, with a comedy receiver and a big dial with finger holes in it, but fitted with modern innards so it can be plugged straight into a normal phone socket.

And, having used it, I now understand why the homes of some of my childhood friends were equipped with telephone tables. Remember those? They had a sort of pouffe arrangement to sit on, a flat surface for the instrument itself, and a drawer for the Yellow Pages.

I thought these people were dead posh. They must have been, if every other requirement of their lives was already so well furnished that they could afford a dedicated piece just for telephoning. But now I realise that the telephone table evolved simply because dialling was so bloody tiring.

Come round and try it if you don't believe me. You have to insert your finger in the hole corresponding to each individual number, haul it around to the little stop, and then wait for it to return to the start ready for the next one. It takes ages. In its favour, the size of your phone bill is automatically limited by the amount of damage your index finger can sustain.

And it's got worse. In 1976 my parents' phone number featured eight digits. Now it has eleven. Doesn't sound like much of a difference, but two of the new ones are noughts, and the nought is right at the beginning of the dial. In the time it takes to whir its way back to first position I can sense my beard growing.

It only takes a few seconds longer to dial with the old phone than it does with the new push-button type, but in this day and age it feels like a month.

Dialling is not the only thing that has speeded up in my lifetime. Data retrieval is another. If, when I was a student, I needed to look up some facts or figures, I had to get up, have a shower, get dressed, put some shoes on, walk to the library, sign in, look up the book I needed in a card index, find it, find the information I wanted, write it down on a piece of paper, walk all the way back to my house and fall into a coma of exhaustion. Now, of course, I can just look up whatever I need on the internet. And yet I become incandescent with impatience if the time taken for the page to render on the screen is much more than the twinkling of an eye.

When I mentally tot up all the time saved in a typical life through the good offices of things that are now much quicker – phones, computers, microwaves, dishwashers, self-service supermarket checkouts, cash machines, drive-through restaurants and so on – I end up wondering why we haven't all become concert pianists in the eternity of leisure time we must have. But we haven't, because we've filled it with other things, and all of them are still, in truth, too slow.

Here we arrive at the real problem of the car. It's not pollution or congestion, or even the cost of the thing. The problem is that cars are creakingly pedestrian by the standards of everything else we do. They're barely faster now than they were when I was a child. Meanwhile, even tin openers are geared for higher speeds now than they were in the 70s. And that's still not fast enough.

Last weekend, for example, I drove to see an old mate who lives in Devon. The journey took three hours. Three hours! Three hours looking out of a window at the arse ends of diesel Vectras and the like. There is no other activity in my life on which I spend such lengthy and uninterrupted stretches of my time.

This is why the car will not be the ruin of the world, as some are claiming. Soon, most people will be sick of it entirely, and all because it's too slow to be of any use. Concorde was retired not because it was too noisy or too wasteful of resources or too expensive; it was because it wasn't fast enough. A journey that took only half as long as it did on a 747 was still a lifetime in an age when you can download a whole album in a minute without even having to put your trousers on. The car will be a victim of its own sloth, just as the horse was.

I believe, in fact, that it will be usurped by something that moves through the largely unexploited medium of the air above our heads, and at truly huge speeds. The trip to Devon will then take just a few minutes, leaving plenty of time for piano practice.

But the car will not disappear entirely, and to understand why not you only have to look at Britain's canals. I doubt that any coal or jute is being moved on them nowadays, because canals, too, eventually became too slow. But canals are being reopened all the time, and they are all full of gaily painted narrowboats crewed by enthusiasts of rustic musical instruments. These people are simply enjoying boating as a hobby.

I'm sure cars will turn into a hobby as well. At the moment it is immoral to price people off the road, because they have no choice in the matter. Most of them would rather not be there anyway. But when the roads are reserved for those who are simply having a laugh, road tax can be raised to £2000 a year to pay for the upkeep. Why not? No one will be forced to drive; they'll be crossing the country at 1000mph in antimatter-powered levitating balls, and then settling down to a few hours of Chopin. In any case, plenty of people spend more than £2000 on golf-club membership or skiing equipment. We can have road pricing, too. When driving is just a game, road pricing will seem no more unreasonable than having to pay to use the pool table in the pub.

Which sort of brings me to the new Porsche 911 Turbo. As a means of getting anywhere quickly, it's just as useless as my Fiat Panda. But imagine how much fun you'll have in a car that powerful when you don't need to be anywhere in particular.

Er, cars are great

I have to admit that I was not initially very enamoured of the basic Skoda Fabia 1.2 five-door. I honestly preferred the minicab that had taken me to the airport at the beginning of the journey, and as the man driving it was the sort of chap who earned a living getting up at 5a.m. to drive someone like me around, you can assume that his life had not gone especially well and that he therefore had a crap car.

But this seemed worse. I was in Andalucia, southern Spain, for recreational reasons and, as usual, had hired a car at Seville airport. I always go for the most basic bracket, because I'm a bit tight and I prefer to spend my holiday pocket money on tapas and *platos combinados*. And as a regular customer of vehicle group A I enjoy the delicious moment of doubt when I wonder if I'll get a Clio (which I like) or a small Peugeot (which I don't).

Still – it's only a hire car and, as P.J. O'Rourke famously observed, few things handle with such aplomb. I would add that there is no other vehicle in the world that inspires less concern for the longevity of its tyres or the condition of its valve train.

But here's the first thing that always strikes me. If I borrow the most basic version of a small hatchback from its manufacturer – for the purpose of road testing, say – it's never as basic as the one I get at an airport. Maybe a special low-spec edition is built for hire car companies whose clients, they know, will always drive it in the spirit Enzo Ferrari intended. Maybe manufacturers always sneak in a few small extras that make what is purportedly the 'entry level model' seem so much nicer than it really is – optional upholstery in a bright colour scheme, some electric windows in the back, a nicer gearknob, perhaps?

Either way, no matter how firm you are with the salesman, regardless of how far you've stretched your meagre car-buying budget, and even if you're one of those people who believes adamantly that a car is just something to take you from A to B, you will struggle to leave a Skoda showroom with a Fabia as boggo as the one I was driving. It looked as though it had fallen off the production line before it had reached the end.

The interior, for example, was finished in the following complementary hues: grey. The carpets were some sort of underlay. The wheel trims were made from the leftover linings of Christmas-biscuit family assortment tins, and the tailgate from the tin itself. The wheel rim was hard and the facia was the single biggest injection moulding in the long history of plastic. I hated it just sitting there.

Then I drove it. Hated it, because it was of course a diesel. Except that at the first refill, when the diesel nozzle wouldn't fit in the filler neck and the symbol of a green pump mocked me from the inside of the flap, I had to acknowledge that it wasn't. This only increased my rage. The steering was definitely too light, the suspension was too bouncy, and all the stations on the radio were in Spanish, although this wasn't necessarily Skoda's fault.

So the first hundred miles or so of the trip, from Seville to the ancient city of Córdoba, was really a protracted and largely unprintable first drive delivered solely for the benefit of Woman, who at the end of it hated me as much as I did the car. At the hotel, I handed the keys and whatever their equivalent of a shilling is to the bellboy and told him I didn't want to see the Skoda again until it was time to go home.

But of course, after a few days of looking at local historic buildings and admiring the trees, it was suggested that a drive through the Sierra Nevada might be nice. I didn't actually think so, but you know how it is, so the Fabia was dragged out and again refilled, with no less astonishment, with unleaded.

Off we went on the main road leading south to Granada, a steady stream of words that don't appear in the Collins English/Spanish Pocket Gem dictionary flowing from the open driver's window like discarded orange peel. I still didn't like it.

Then we turned off onto smaller side roads through typical southern European villages, where men sit in plastic chairs on the pavement all day and signs warn of the Bandos Señoras, the traditional Andalucian Bandit Girls, who run wild on the plains and hold up unwary travellers with ornamental souvenir *espadas*. Finally, and mapless, we entered the mountains themselves.

And now something strange happened. Gradually, imperceptibly, and no matter how I tried to resist it, the Fabia slowly began to endear itself to me. I looked forward to long hills, where I could push the gruff little engine and rejoice in its willing grumble. I threw it gaily into tortuous and badly engineered bends that had probably evolved out of the footpaths trodden by weary Moorish settlers hundreds of years ago. As the day wore on, and we became more lost, the pleasure of simply driving gradually usurped my former dissatisfaction with the car itself.

This happens to me now and then, but probably not often enough; that sudden sense that simply being allowed to have something as amazing as a car is a truly mind-blowing privilege. How can it be that for such a tiny outlay at the Seville airport rent-a-car concourse I can end up as some sort of latter-day caliph presiding over a whole range of mountains and its ancient forts? Who'd have thought it, eh?

And I end up thinking that we might have got the whole car thing wrong; that we have turned them into monuments to possession and lost sight of what we can actually do with them, which is climb aboard outside our front doors and, if we keep going long enough, arrive at the other side of the world.

Yes, the Ferrari F430 Spider would have been more exciting than the Fabia, but the gap between them is a mere fissure compared with the yawning chasm between the Fabia and no car at all.

The car – any sort of car – is still, and despite what its detractors say, one of the greatest adventures open to us. And to the bored man who picked me up from home in his ancient Rover 600, I'm tempted to say sell everything, chuck in the minicabbing job, and go for a proper drive.

Brochure rage, part I

A few weeks back, I decided it was time to replace the ancient radio and CD player that stands on a shelf in my kitchen, and which, as you can imagine, is my constant companion during the long hours of parmesan-shaving and mixed-leaf-tossing.

The CD player had developed a digital stutter, which could turn even a recording of Bach's St Matthew Passion into gangsta rap, and in a fit of unfed pique, Fusker, the world's most ill-mannered cat, had headbutted one of the little speakers onto the floor, shattering its delicate innards and rendering the output something less than true stereo.

Anyway, I've always fancied one of those Bang & Olufsen radio and multi-CD jobs, the one in which five discs are loaded in a strip and automatically slot themselves into place; a true digital successor to the electro-mechanical marvel that was the Seeburg jukebox. I know hi-fi buffs dismiss this sort of thing as a fashion accessory rather than a true music system, but they're still lamenting the passing of the valve. So I went out and picked up a brochure.

Nice. Very funky cylindrical blue speakers oddly redolent in the shape of the BMW Munich headquarters building. Soft, blinking red lights, remote control and opportunities for wall-mounting in a number of orientations. On such a system, I'd enjoy watching the collected Scott Joplin slide into position almost as much as I'd enjoy listening to it.

But something was wrong. The text didn't seem to talk that

much about sound and function, instead concentrating on a florid explanation of how stylish the B&O was, and what it said about me. There was an image of a man in something approaching a black poloneck – one of those freewheeling and loft-dwelling guru types, I fear – and then there was a gratuitous picture of an Audi A8. There was no reason for it to be there that I could see. It was just an A8 that had been parked in the wrong leaflet.

Now I admire Audis, but I find them a bit pretentious. It's that whole drive-an-Audi-and-be-in-touch-with-the-contemporary-design-zeitgeist thing. And that, I think, was why it was in the B&O brochure; because the sort of person who buys a B&O radiogram is the sort of person who would feel good about driving an Audi. That is, a bit of a square.

So I binned the B&O booklet and bought a radio/CD player made by Roberts who, according to the box, also make radios for the Queen, who is the sort of woman who stores her cornflakes in a Tupperware tub and therefore must be OK. The Roberts is great, comes with a prosaic instruction book, and is exactly the sort of radio for a man who only wanted a radio.

This is not the first time an excess of lifestyle imagery has turned me away from a product that I might otherwise have liked. Years ago, when I bought my house, there were some new riverside apartments being built nearby. So I went to have a look.

Like a Spanish hotel, they weren't yet finished, but that was OK because I knew the wooden hoarding around the site would be liberally adorned with pictures to tempt the prospective buyer into the forthcoming show apartment. And there they were.

Not one of them showed me what I wanted to see, such as the floor plan, the prices, the view from the upper floors, or whether or not the khazi had a window. Instead there were images of people with perfect cheekbones talking on mobile telephones, or looking at laptops in absurd places, or returning

from the shops having just spent a fortune on designer spectacles and haircuts. It was all about as much use as a chocolate
Maserati.

And almost certainly fatuous nonsense, of course. But what
if it were true? I couldn't possibly buy one of these flats in case
I ended up living among people who had just moved out of a
brochure, and who might keep me awake all night with the
racket from their B&O stereos.

Good, solid product information is in danger of being totally
usurped by subliminal images that seem designed to remind
me that I'm not a male model or successful and high-flying
executive. It comes with every consumer product on the shelf.
I can't even buy an apple from Sainsbury's without being
assaulted by a huge poster showing some grinning idiot whose
life and teeth seem to have been immeasurably enhanced by
eating one.

Can't buy a car, either. This week, I've been looking at the
new Aston Martin V8 Vantage Roadster. Again, I liked the look
of it and so, as a fantasist, picked up a brochure.

God in heaven it made me cross.

To be continued . . .

Old bag dies after 25 years as my friend

At the base of the great pyramid of possession is my house, with all that a man may want therein and, as age advances, more. A spice rack (a present, that), books unopened for years, shoes, slightly too much furniture for the space, that Anglepoise lamp with the limp mechanism that I'll mend one day.

Not all of it strictly necessary, I know, because if I go away on a long trip I can condense the essence of my existence into the two Globetrotters that sit on top of the wardrobe, plus a carry-on bag for so-called 'valuables'. The things that make it to the cases must be those that I really need. Or are they?

It follows that what really matters in life is only that which will fit into my Adidas motorcycling backpack. It's no holdall, this, because it won't all go in. It is the bag of truth, to luggage what a rifle is to an American Marine. This is my Adidas backpack. There are many like it, but this one is mine. And I've had it for as long as I can remember; since long before I ever rode a motorcycle. So long, in fact, that it has completed two revolutions of the wheel of fashion, and local youths the age I was when I bought it, and who were then as yet unborn, have pronounced it 'cool'.

It's a simple backpack from an earlier age. It has just two compartments: the main one, for pants, socks, a T-shirt or two and the soft shoes that go on when the biking boots come off, and a small one, for the wallet, the passport, and those other things that lesser travellers might put in something called a 'bum bag'. Once, it was stuffed with trainers and sweatshirts and was heaved with a sigh over the shoulder of a reluctant teenage sportsman. But then it became the bag I took on the bike.

And though the bikes have come and gone, the bag has endured. I have rarely been on a bike without my old backpack. It has crossed the continent with me on something big, its weight on my back a measure of my true worth and a reassuring reminder that the demon of acquisition has been renounced, if only temporarily. To the amateur motorcyclist on a long trip, a small backpack is as liberating as the machine itself.

But it might just as easily have served as a shopping basket, and I have fed six people with the volume of groceries Mr Dazzler deemed I should be able to transport on the humble Honda 90. There has always been a piece of onion skin and some earth in the bottom of the backpack, there to confirm that it is a microcosm of home that I carry behind me, snail-like.

But now it's broken. The end, inevitably, was ignominious. I stuffed one more thing into it, pulled on the zip and it was rent asunder like the curtains in the Temple. In that moment I was suffused with the deep melancholy that comes when some physical link with an earlier existence crumples before you, instantly consigning half a lifetime to memory alone. When the bag burst, a past that I had managed to drag behind me suddenly began to recede.

I have taken the loss of my Adidas backpack very badly, as you can probably tell. Of course I would, because the bond that exists between a man and his bag is a precious thing understood by many – explorers, soldiers, flying doctors, steeplejacks. But it has never been expressed better than it was by Ernest K. Gann in *Fate is the Hunter,* an autobiographical account of his life as an airline and air transport pilot. His flight bag, bought new at the start of his career, was the only constant in his life, and its gradual decay marked the passage of his itin-erant living until the point when it disintegrated and he knew it was time to stop. 'I loved that bag,' he says. Love! For a bag! But I know what he means.

I've bought a new biking bag now, a modern thing made by Alpinestars, a sort of 'by bikers, for bikers' type of thing. And, as with people who buy a new car only every twenty years and are astonished by electric windows, I'm amazed at how the backpack has come on. It's a better shape and more comfort-able, being moulded closer to the spine's desire. It has better zips, more compartments, effective waterproofing, more easily adjustable straps, stronger material. It is a superior product in every single way.

Give me a couple of decades and I might even come to like it.

Triples all round

Regular readers may remember that, some weeks back, I promised myself a new Triumph Speed Triple motorcycle if I could throw three treble 20s on the local pub dartboard.

I'd been working reasonably hard, putting a bit aside, renouncing the devil that sat on my shoulder and taunted me with talk of stair carpet, and generally honouring my Protestant upbringing. Save now, spend later; neither a lender nor a borrower be, do not fall into the clutches of Mammon by buying on the tick.

Anyway, last week, on a particularly quiet Tuesday evening in the Cross Keys, I finally did it. Despite the new telly mounted on a wall bracket midway between the oche and the raddled blackboard, positioned only a few inches above the ideal treble-20 trajectory and therefore a bit off-putting, I was rewarded with the satisfying thunk of three arrows piercing the virgin red rectangle denoting the highest score on the board.

It's a pity that, as with so many holes-in-one and prize-winning pike, no one else was there to see it. I was the only customer. Even the landlady had temporarily disappeared into the cellar and, when she re-emerged a few seconds later, could only stare in disbelief at a grouping never before seen in the pub's 150-year history. There have been at least five previous boards since I've been a regular, and each has been committed to the skip in the sobering knowledge that the treble 20 has been a waste of good bristle.

What a great bike. Ugly and pugnacious, perhaps, but in a well-bred sort of way, like Raffles the Gentleman Thug in *Viz*. I'd forgotten what an appealing layout the transverse triple is. A single thuds, a V-twin clatters, and the ubiquitous in-line four simply blends with that aural backdrop that is all the four-cylinder cars out there. But the triple has a slight irregularity to it – a murmur of mechanical dissent, almost – which produces a fabulously resonant and gravelly exhaust note. It's like riding around on Lee Marvin.

The Trumpet has been declared by many reputable motorcycling magazines to be the best and most capable of the naked big-bore streetbikes. Mind you, the Slazenger racket owned by my schoolmate Lonny was generally regarded as the finest tennis weapon a 14-year-old could possibly be given by an ambitious parent. The notoriety he earned from having one was second only to that he enjoyed for his embarrassing incompetence on the tennis court.

Similarly, I once played saxophone in a jazz band that included a bloke called George, who had a rare and very valuable electric guitar. Everyone was very impressed with George's guitar, but rather less so with George's abilities on it. When the programme for our next gig was produced, it listed saxophonists, trombonists, a pianist and a bassist. But George appeared as a 'guitar owner'.

The fact remains that I'm still not really that good at riding motorcycles, and certainly nowhere near as good as my new bike would suggest. This is why I won't be campaigning the Speed Triple in this year's Thundersprint meeting. Once again, organiser Frank Melling* has cajoled me into taking part, mainly by filling in the forms on my behalf and then sending me my race number.

Daily Telegraph classic motorcycling correspondent and accomplished cake decorator.

Yes, the Thundersprint is a race meeting, a sprint contest. You can find out all about it by looking it up on what in Frank's neck of the woods is known as 'tinternet'. The course is short and tortuous, and the hay bales are very close to the track. A torquey, short-wheelbase and famously agile bike like the Speed Triple ought to do quite well on it, having the grip to allow the rider to 'get it right over' (as Rocket Ron Haslam would say) and the grunt to power out of the bends and down the short straight sections. So if you owned a Speed Triple but couldn't actually ride it properly, the whole thing could have been designed with the express aim of making you look a right donkey and like a bloke with all the gear and no idea.

I've therefore entered my 1964 Honda 90, a bike with a top speed of around 45mph, perhaps twenty of which might be attained on the opening straight. Hopefully the good-natured weekend crowd will applaud the self-deprecation of the bloke with the comically small motorcycle and absurdly large crash helmet.

He'll come last, as usual, but then he would, wouldn't he? Look at his bike.

Rolls-Royce – no longer a car for clowns

I may have done a bad thing. Using man maths, I've bought a car, having put another of my cars up for sale, while assuming it's worth more than I'll actually get for it, obviously, because that's how the books balance.

And it's even worse than that, because the car I'm selling is my dearly beloved Bentley T2. The one I've already bought is a fixed-head Rolls-Royce Corniche. Not only has the Rolls cost more than I imagine the Bentley is worth; once I've factored in the real value of the Bentley I'll also have to contribute the money I think I still have from selling a Triumph motorcycle four years ago, even though I spent that on a piano.

According to one or two of my mates, however, the arithmetic is the least of my problems. 'What?' said one. 'A Rolls-Royce? Won't you look like an ageing northern comedian?' I hadn't really thought of that. In fact, I hadn't really considered the image issue at all.

Confining our investigation, for the moment, to the two cars in question, I think there is a good case for the Rolls. The Silver Shadow and T-series saloons always looked better with the rounded Bentley grille up front, even though that, and the shape of the bonnet, is the only difference between them. Somehow, though, the two-door Corniche, though very closely related, looks more proper with that scale model of the Parthenon on the nose. Can't explain why; it just does.

The colour scheme of the Corniche is better, too. It's finished

in the colour of Fitou, and the interior is plain and covered
with an indistinct pale-beige hide. Now I once met a man with
a condition known as synaesthesia, for whom things that you
or I might regard as having shape, colour or texture manifested
themselves as tastes. All Peugeots tasted of old fabric, and he
could never own a Porsche because they combined Marmite
with bananas and made him feel unwell. I was never really
able to grasp this until I saw the Corniche, which immediately
invokes a cheese and wine evening of the contemporary era,
which was 1972. The Bentley, from 1980, is light metallic blue
with a blue-piped creamy cabin, so looks like one of the star
cars in *Boogie Nights*.

But what of the broader question of this thing called 'brand
image'? It's undoubtedly true that over the last few decades the
Rolls-Royce marque has suffered something of an credibility
problem. By the late 90s R-R had become so undeniably nouveau
that there was a case for replacing Sykes' Spirit of Ecstasy mascot
with a gilded figurine of one of the Jimmies Saville or Tarbuck.
Bentley, through the use of turbochargers and by exploiting its
race heritage stuff and alluding to chaps in taches, had been
transformed into the carriage of choice for the discerning enthusiast, or something like that. But now I'm not so sure.

Let's get one thing absolutely straight: the toffs aren't buying
either of them. They're all broke, and busy flogging the
Rembrandts to pay off the staff and keep them quiet. Posh cars
are bought by rap stars and new-media entrepreneurs, so there's
no point in being hung up about breeding.

If anything, I reckon Bentleys have become the more bling
of the two. The Continental GT is too cheap to be truly exclusive, and take a look at the wheels on the Arnage T. There's
more rubber in the suspension of a 70s model. Rolls-Royce, now
a separate concern again, looks a bit more louche and can be
had with snakeskin-effect interior door panels. But Simon
Cowell has one. Two, possibly. And apparently 50Cent had one
and sawed the roof off.

So what have I actually done to my self-esteem by trading a Bentley for a Rolls-Royce? As it turns out, absolutely nothing. There's a huge amount of old cock talked about 'the badge' and 'the brand', but taking this sort of thing seriously is nothing more than an admission that you don't know what you're on about. What I actually admire, in the end, is cars that were built in the Crewe factory and its Mulliner Park Ward subsidiary. All Rolls-Royce and Bentley models of the 70s and 80s are exactly the same bar a few detail trim differences; they were made by the same people to the same standard, which was a very high one, and to imagine that each says something different about you is utterly facile. They say a great deal about their creators, not their owners. We are merely celebrating it.

As real aristocrats, when we still had them, were fond of saying: those who mind don't matter. And those who matter don't mind.

A modernist's guide to the Goodwood Revival

I realise I'm a bit late with this, but I wanted to say what a smashing time I and my car-bore chums had at this year's Goodwood Revival. Great cars stretching as far as the eye could see was pretty good in itself, but there were also eight Spitfires in the air at one time and, best of all, I finally had the chance, after some thirty-five years of waiting, to meet Raymond Baxter; a man who in my opinion, and for his commentary on the Farnborough Airshow alone, should be Sir Raymond Baxter and bar.

I've never been to the revival before, only the Festival of Speed. The Festival is a merely a series of timed romps up the (admittedly very long) driveway of Goodwood House, but the revival takes place on the circuit that nearly killed Stirling Moss and was eventually struck from the Grand Prix calendar for being too dangerous. And here were period cars on pathetic tyres racing for real in the pouring rain.

Of course it rained on the Saturday, but we're British, not Italian, and we don't care. As long as there are carrier bags our plucky public will stick them on their heads and shrug this sort of thing off. In any case, the rain made the racing more dramatic and, as Dr Johnson observed, 'When two Englishmen meet, their first talk is of the weather'. Some trite remark about a downpour is a great way to break the ice with a man about to drown in the cockpit of his 60s Formula One car.

I admit that there are some things about the revival that

make me nervous. It's themed, for example, which means dressing up in 40s and 50s clothing, and I've always believed that anything involving dressing up – such as working for McDonald's or being a high-court judge – should be avoided. Some parts of the infield looked like the set of *It Ain't Half Dad's Army Do 'Ave 'Em Mum.*

But at least it allows you to identify immediately all those who wish either that the war was still on or that they'd been born American, and avoid them instead. Someone pointed out that I'd got the decade wrong and come in 1970s gear, to which I had to point out, gently, that they were just my normal clothes.

The theme of the evening party was 'The Last Days of the Raj', which for most of us meant traditional Indian garb. I've always thought this sort of thing looks pretty pukka on real Indians, but on me and my pals it looked more like an episode of *Carry On Up The Costume Hire Shop.* Fortunately, no one in our party *was* Indian, thus sparing us from another embarrassing these-are-my-normal-clothes incident.

But the cars! C-types, D-types, old Alfas and Maseratis, even a Maybach (from 1946, not the current wheeled branch of Maplins Electronics). It is quite incredible to observe how machines that were once funded by whole industries have become the personal playthings of an old-car elite. The pits abound with toffs, playboys, and investment bankers, which could be exclusive and intimidating anywhere else. But because the heroically foppish Lord March is a gentleman and an egalitarian, we of the shoeless proletariat are allowed to wander the pits, examine and even touch things, and exclaim 'Eeh look at this one our Johnny isn't that a real smasher', or however it was people spoke during the Suez Crisis.

All of this, however, pales into nothingness alongside the achievements of the motorcyclists in the Barry Sheene Memorial Trophy, a celebration of racing bikes from the early 60s run in the pouring rain. They were not all young, and as Mike Haywood (not a bike racer, but Rotherham's own poet) said:

Old age strikes fast
Like rooted trees
And grabs these lads
Below the knees.

But it hadn't got to this lot yet. Superb camerawork on Goodwood's own TV system recorded the elegance with which they tipped Manx Nortons and Matchless G50s into the streaming Woodcote corner; the faultless fluidity of their arm- and legwork in the face of the threat of a certain spill if they got it wrong. I've never ridden any of these old race bikes, but my guess is that they're even trickier to ride than they are to start, and desperately unforgiving. It is often said that a modern car has ten times the computing power of an Apollo space rocket; here was a grid full of machines with less collective computing power than an electric doorbell. But, by crikey, these chaps could ride them.

As a notoriously wobbly motorcyclist, I realised I should be able to do better in the dry on a normal road on a thoroughly modern Yamaha. So the next day I went out, and I did.

That's what I liked most about this event. Revival my 1940s flat hat. It was more of an inspiration.

How the small car will save the car

It's now three years since I've been to the Frankfurt Motor Show, which sounds like a terrible lapse of professionalism but to be honest, I'm quite glad. The Frankfurt Show represents, by some margin, the longest walk a motoring journalist will ever take, and all for the purpose of looking at some cars. So it's not just knackering, it's also strangely ironic. One year, an unfortunate German correspondent actually died on the way round, it was all so gruelling.

For the last two years I've been tied up with the filming of *Top Gear*, and this year, at the last minute, I was required to be elsewhere to give a talk about my new book, *James May's 20th Century*, which I'm delighted to say is on special offer at Woolworths and some supermarkets and a rollicking good read to boot (people like Jilly Cooper get away with this sort of thing, so why shouldn't I?).

However, I sort of wish I'd made it this time, because it's clear from the musings of my colleagues at *Telegraph* Motoring that something is going on: small cars, small engines, small amounts of CO_2, small performance and other things terribly unappealing to small boys, who are the only true and uncorrupted arbiters on such matters. It is beginning to look as though green concerns have finally triumphed, and that this fantastic petrol-soaked party we've been having over the last 100 years is finally winding down. The band is well into the smoochy numbers, some of the chairs have been stacked up, and now the lights are back on everything looks a bit shabby.

So I'm here to tell you not to worry yet. For a start, a lot of it has the ring of cant about it. Mercedes-Benz may talk a good DiesOtto or hydrogen fuel cell, but while no one's been looking they've managed to shoehorn their biggest V8 into the C-class, just to confirm that they haven't lost any of their well-established ability to overdo it. By the time you read this, I'll be driving it.

More to the point, and as I've tried to argue in my new book, *James May's 20th Century*, which is currently available at a discount from some supermarkets and far easier to digest than many products at twice the price, small, slow cars are more important than big, fast ones. Small cars are more fun for more of the people more of the time, and if they didn't exist, neither would the posh stuff.

Furthermore, and as I might have gone on to say in *James May's 20th Century**** if I'd been this cross when I was writing it, building a small, low-priced, spacious, fuel-efficient and crash-worthy car is a much more testing engineering proposition than building a 500 horsepower supercar for £200,000. I can't actually prove this, but conversations with car engineers who have tried both suggest it's true. Every few years some nutcase with an old industrial unit announces that he is going to build the ultimate uncompromised megacar, because Ferrari and Porsche are somehow getting it all wrong. These people never attempt to build an £8000 80mpg city car. Why? Because that's far too difficult.

It amuses me, then, that the anti-car lobby and misguided ecologists think that they are sounding the death knell of any car more elaborate than my Fiat Panda. Nothing could be further from the truth. Public pressure and government initiatives to cap a manufacturer's overall across-the-range CO_2

---

*On special offer in Woolworths and some supermarkets.

output will almost certainly force the development of clever small cars, but as a result of that the whole business of car-making will be in ruder health than ever. If they can get those cars right, they can do anything, and when the small cars are good, the big ones tend to be better.

I could go further. In fact, I shall. I suspect that creating a truly fabulous car is a task best discharged by those who have proved themselves with stuff for the masses. It explains why Ford came to trounce Ferrari at Le Mans. Remember, too, that the Porsche 911 would never have existed without the Beetle before it, and that the automotive might of Japan was founded largely on K-class runabouts that were barely more sophisticated than the cyclecars of the 1920s.

Consider this: the fastest, rarest, most expensive and most technologically replete supercar to date has been built by a company that was named for the people's everyday need simply to get about. Of course, they bought another badge to put on it, but everyone knows that the Bugatti Veyron is a Volkswagen. And it's all the better for it.

Relax. Pour yourself another pint of petrol. It's not over yet.